THE

STORY

ECONOMY

*"How to Use the Power of Story
In your Marketing Funnel to
Attract and Keep more Customers"*

———————

Tom J. Curtis

THE STORY ECONOMY
Copyright © 2014 by Tom J. Curtis
www.StoryEconomy.com

ISBN 978-1499521931

Printed in USA

Dedication

For Melissa and our kids,
Nothing I do really matters without them.
Thank you for your patience and support.
Luv!

Table of Contents

Book Bonuses

Throughout this book, I mention book bonuses that I have created that are available to you for free as a thank you for purchasing and reading my book. As the book evolves even after publishing, I will continue to add new bonuses to help you tell a remarkable story with your business and develop the systems for sharing it.

You can gain access to the book bonuses at:

www.StoryEconomy.com

Endorsement

Tom has nailed it. If you don't quite "get" the way business is done in the new online economy, then this is the book that will open your eyes. Who needs this book? You do, unless you are already successfully telling your story online in such a way that it DRIVES a steady stream of eager prospects into a well thought out funnel system of products and content 24X7. Even IF you are already doing that, this book will sharpen your sword. I give it my highest recommendation.

Jim Cockrum
www.JimCockrum.com

A Quick Thought

When the late Steve Jobs co-founded Apple Computer in 1976, he did not have dreams of opening a shop and selling a few hundred computers to tech geeks around Northern California. He did not think of what office chair he should buy or what kind of file cabinet would look good in the corner.

It started in a garage where Steve Jobs had dreams of telling an amazing story, and he told that story through Apple, Inc. and all the revolutionary products that sprang forth.

If office chairs and filing cabinets were not part of an amazing story for Steve Jobs, why does it seem to be the story that millions of other entrepreneurs tell every day? The truth is, nobody will ever remember the story about the business cards you picked out, the features of your products, or whether or not your desk chair had lumbar support.

People remember amazing, remarkable stories! They remember when their lives transformed and when they felt a connection...and they feel that connection through stories.

The stories you tell with your business can be remarkable or they can be forgotten. Remarkable stories change the world...even from a garage.

Here's where I'm going with that...

Introduction

"Every once in a while a revolutionary product comes along that changes everything."
    -Steve Jobs

Sometimes a revolutionary company comes along that changes everything! Apple Computer changed everything in 1976, when Steve Jobs and Steve Wozniak founded the company that would tell us a captivating story with revolutionary products.

The story was never just about the products, but about the stories the products would tell in the lives of the consumers. Steve Jobs had a vision of what that story would be and he continued to tell and share it until the final days of his life in October 2011.

A Remarkable Story

It is easy to see when a business and the entrepreneur in front of it intend to tell a remarkable story. That is the one thing about a business, it is either telling a remarkable story that is going to be remembered or a forgettable story that is easily forgotten.

There are plenty of businesses out there that we buy from whose purpose is to engage with us, cultivate a long-lasting relationship, and sell us amazing products.

There are also too many businesses out there that are doing just the opposite, telling stupid and forgettable stories of disappointment.

The good news is that it does not have to be that way for those businesses. They can choose at any time to tell a better story and create a devoted following of loyal customers.

When I started my own roofing company in 2002, I was not the best entrepreneur out there or the most gifted businessman, by any means. I did, however, have an overwhelming desire to tell a great story as an entrepreneur with my business. I was determined to dispel the negative stereotype many people have about dealing with contractors.

That paid off for me in many ways and not just financially. I built long-lasting relationships with my clients who were condominium homeowner association board members and property managers. In fact, I even stepped away from the business back in 2006 to pursue other business ventures, and when I came back in 2008, I easily found work again and grew my company a second time through the relationships I had built and the story I told with my business.

You can choose to tell a Remarkable Story

You can choose to tell a remarkable story with your business. There are just a few essential tweaks in your mindset and the right system that is necessary for creating and telling the type of story that attracts people to you and your company. That is really what it is all about anyway, attracting people to your business and keeping them as customers.

In this book you will read about entrepreneurs and their businesses that tell remarkable stories. You will learn the mindset that is necessary for telling your story in your marketplace and the system to use to tell that story.

I will share tactics and tools that have helped me and other successful entrepreneurs with the strategy of telling remarkable stories with our businesses.

If there is one thing I wish for you to take away from this book, it is this: That you will commit to telling a remarkable story as an entrepreneur, like Steve Jobs did, and that you will implement a system that continues to tell your story seamlessly to your customers for many years to come.

We are all in 'The Story Economy' together. We are entrepreneurs leading the way for others to follow. Let's leave them clues and success stories to capitalize on. That is what my purpose is, to create more entrepreneurs that commit to telling remarkable stories. I believe that most, if not all, of the world's problems can and will be solved by entrepreneurs.   We are problem-solving trailblazers leading the way to new innovations and solutions. We are inventors, innovators, producers, and thought leaders that will always find a way.

I am happy that you have joined me on this journey.

Welcome to The Story Economy!

Chapter 1

The Remarkable Story Mindset

Telling a remarkable story with your business begins with developing the right mindset. In the construction industry, I have encountered far too many business owners with the mindset that the customer does not matter, that showing up on time in a clean, professional way is not a big deal, and that following through with their promises and providing top-quality workmanship is an after-thought.

At the same time, I am also encountering businesses where it is apparent that telling a remarkable story is first and foremost in the mind of the owners. It is a mindset that is developed from the beginning and passed down to the entire organization.

There are three (3) key questions a business owner must answer to develop a remarkable story mindset.

1. Why Does My Business Matter?

People don't buy what you do; they buy why you do it.
- Simon Sinek, author of Start with Why

Several years ago and many times since, I have read this question in various publications and books, *"Why does your business matter?"* It is one of the most important and powerful questions an entrepreneur can and should be asking from the very beginning as well as all the way through the life of his or her business.

As a commercial roofing contractor of my own business it was easy for me to answer that question. My business mattered because the story my business was telling was different. Early on I had chosen to adopt the mindset that my business mattered to my clients. Most of them had experienced mediocre contractors so I knew I could come in and tell a better story and get the work I wanted.

Any business owner can do that. Even the smallest tweak in the mindset can create huge changes. Deciding to do something that matters can make all the difference in the world.

Creating Something that Matters

In 2002, Blake Mycoskie was competing with his sister on the television reality show, *The Amazing Race*, in Argentina. When Blake returned to Argentina while on vacation in 2006, he noticed some polo players wearing a simple slip-on shoe made of canvas called alpargatas. It turned out that farmers had worn these simple shoes for hundreds of years. Also while on vacation, Blake noticed when he was doing some volunteer work in Buenos Aires, that many of the children running around were not wearing any shoes. This led Blake to the idea of introducing a version of the alpargata shoes to the North American market. But what's amazing and truly remarkable about this story is that not only did Blake Mycoskie introduce a great, new shoe to the market, he also decided that for every pair of shoes he sold, he would donate one pair of shoes to the shoeless youth in Argentina and other developing countries.

TOMS shoes was soon introduced along with the slogan, *'One for One'*. For TOMS, which stands for Tomorrow's Shoes, it was never just about selling shoes. It was about putting shoes on the feet of children who did not have shoes. TOMS was just the catalyst for doing it.

Blake Mycoskie knew his *'why'*. It was not about what he was doing; it was about why he was doing it. Blake sold shoes so shoeless kids could have shoes. Today, you can see people everywhere wearing a pair of TOMS shoes and know that another pair of shoes is protecting the feet of a child somewhere out in the world.

In 2012, Blake wrote a book called, *Start Something that Matters*. Without a clear *'why'*, there was no way Blake could have written a meaningful book like that to tell his story of TOMS and what he set out to do with it.

Intentions are Good

I do not believe anyone ever sets out on the entrepreneurial path to start something that sucks. I believe we all have good intentions in the beginning and a lot of entrepreneurs follow those intentions to their graves.

Steve Jobs, as brash and bold as he was, set out to change the world and kept his eye single to that intention until he was no longer with us. I benefit from Steve's intention every day, including right now as I write this book from my Apple laptop computer.

When I was 19 years old, I started a window washing business. I bought some supplies and went out looking for my first customer. My Dad had a rich friend at the time and she agreed to be my first window-washing customer. So I went to my new customer's house and counted all her windows and gave her a price of about $100 to wash all the windows in her house. I swear it felt like there were a thousand windows and there might as well have been. It took me a week to wash all those windows! I thought I was going to die! That may have been the only time I was ever unhappy depositing a check.

However, in the beginning, I had good intentions. I was going to provide a quality service to my customers at a fair price...mostly fair to them. But as I started that job with my first customer, my intentions shifted and I began to plot my escape from the hell I had created for myself. Luckily, I escaped after that first customer and pursued other business ventures.

You see, back when I was 19, I had no idea who I was or why I was doing anything.

My point is that a lot of business owners start out with good intentions and maybe even a clear 'why', but over time they seem to lose sight of what that 'why' was. I believe this happens because they do not have a clear picture of the story they are going to tell with their business or a system for telling it. They do not envision their customer as a hero in that story and how they will always find new ways to keep the hero happy and loyal by improving the story they are in. They forget about what matters.

Getting ready to tell a Story

I can remember several years ago having a conversation with my Dad as I was starting my roofing business. I was both excited and really freaked out about starting my own business. My wife and I had a new baby boy and I had just moved us all back to Southern California from Las Vegas, Nevada so I could start my new roofing company in a prime location that had just enough rain to make things interesting.

There were a lot of things on my mind back then, like getting the right business cards and having everything in place before I really did anything like actually talk to any prospects.

My Dad said something very profound to me during our conversation. He said a lot of people, when they first get into business, try to get everything perfect before they actually open their doors and start doing business. They want the right desk and chair, stationary, computer, wall color, etc. He said that these people get stuck in the process of getting ready to do business. He then went on to say that a lot of nonsense goes on in the beginning and that people do not realize that they are in business until they have customers.

It was not hard for me to immediately grasp what he was saying. I realized I was stuck in the process of getting ready to do business. Lots of people fall into this trap for many different reasons, but for me, it was fear. However, the fear of being broke was even greater so I set out to find myself some customers.

When entrepreneurs are stuck in the process of getting ready to do business, they are stuck in the process of getting ready to tell their story. It is easy to get stuck in this process. It happens in the beginning and can happen at any time during the life of a business.

I suppose it's the nervousness of doing something for the first time like riding a bike, hitting a baseball, playing the lead in a theater production, or stepping to the open door of an airplane as you prepare to skydive for the first time. It is the fear of the unknown.

There is only so much preparation a new entrepreneur needs to accomplish before opening his or her business. After that, he or she is simply stuck in the process of getting ready. If your business is going to matter, stop getting ready to tell your story and start telling it. Sooner or later you just need to stick your foot out, take a step, and put your story out there so we can be a part of it.

Does your business matter in your marketplace?

It's time to answer that question for yourself. The life of your business depends on it. Does it really matter to your customers? The best indication as to whether or not your business matters is if you are referred to the friends and family of your existing customers. If not, then it's time to find out how to make your business and story matter in your marketplace. It's time to develop the right mindset that matters.

The quote at the beginning of this chapter is so crucial to creating a story that matters.

'People don't buy what you do; they buy why you do it.'

WHY you are in business and **WHY** you do what you do is what matters. Find out why and you'll find what matters.

Making a Commitment

The difference between involvement and commitment is like ham and eggs. The chicken is involved; the pig is committed.
   -*Martina Navratilova*

In the year 1519, a Spaniard named, Hernán Cortés, sailed to the Americas to advance the territorial reach of Spain by attacking the Aztec Empire.

The more inspiring and short version of the story continues like this:

Upon his arrival, Cortés proceeded to set fire to three of the four ships that he and his conquistadors set sail in. One ship was preserved in order for Cortés to send his bounty back to Spain.

It is said that Cortés burned the ships to show his men that there was no going back.   It was move forward and conquer, or die trying.

Apparently the stunt worked and Cortés did conquer the Aztec Empire, thus establishing further Spanish influence on the American continent.

The Cortés story is a story of commitment. Thomas Edison was committed to inventing the light bulb and failed thousands of times in the process.   However, he was committed and eventually was successful in lighting up the world.

When you purposely sever the path to a forgettable story you are committed to a remarkable one.

To tell a remarkable story with your business, you have to be committed to doing so.   That commitment is a commitment to your customers. Everything your business does has to be about the customers. Anything less just will not cut it and you will end up telling a stupid story.

When you commit and act upon your commitment to creating an amazing story with your business, you are burning your ships just as Cortés did.

There is no going back because to do so, would mean the death of your business. When your story is remarkable, your customers will notice. They will like the way they feel in your story and going back from that would be like Cortés trying to go back to Spain without his ships. Drowning would surely be the result.

The Fence

Are you familiar with the metaphor about sitting on the fence? You know how it goes...you are kind of sitting on the fence between two different choices and you do not know which one to choose?

Here is an analogy to explain it. Let's say you are trying to choose between eating healthy food and eating junk food. You know that eating healthy food will improve your health, make your clothes fit better, and allow you to live longer. But you just love your junk food and you are not sure about giving it up. You are sitting on the fence unsure of which path to choose.

Let me make it easy for you.

The fence is a lie!

It's a myth!

It's an illusion!

It's a phantom!

It DOES NOT exist. It is an invisible barrier you have created in your mind that gives you a reason to choose to continue eating the junk food. It's the same thing with good and evil...if you will permit my philosophical overtone. If you are sitting on the fence deciding between good and evil, you are still choosing evil.

As a kid, I was a crazy Star Wars fan. I loved it when Yoda counseled Luke Skywalker by saying, "Do or do not!" There is no try!

How many times has that line been quoted over the years, right?

Yoda was wise. Again, you must choose to commit to telling a meaningful story, otherwise you are choosing a stupid story.

Raising the Bar

Athletes that compete in the high jump are constantly attempting to raise the bar they are jumping over. When they are competing, raising the bar means they have set a mark for the other athletes to try and clear. If one athlete sets a mark, it becomes pointless for the other athletes to jump anything lower as anything lower would be mediocre.

I saw a Nike ad once that said, *"You don't win silver; you lose gold."*

Is there any athlete that goes to the Olympics planning to win a silver medal? Does any athlete train to be second best? In the same way, do you want your business to be the second best in your industry or are you going to be the one raising the bar?

Apple raises the bar every time they introduce a new product.

There are lots of companies that commit to telling remarkable stories and at the same time they raise the bar and say to their competitors, *"Try and beat that!"*

One company who is raising the bar is Chipotle. Chipotle is an all-natural, Mexican fast food chain. I have eaten there several times and the food is terrific. Now, it's not the best Mexican food I have ever eaten, but something about the story they tell keeps me coming back for more.

Chipotle recently teamed up with Academy Award-winning, Moonbot Studios, to create a short animated film about a scarecrow that goes to work every day in a giant factory that genetically modifies food and animals for consumption.

In the film the scarecrow goes to work and repairs a large sign on the side of the factory that says *'all-natural'*, but before he attaches the board back to the sign, he peeks through the opening and sees a machine injecting chickens with steroid-like hormones that instantly bloats them up.

Next, the scarecrow zooms to the top of the factory to repair the side of an enormous black and white metal cow. As the scarecrow looks inside the cow, he sees hundreds of cows in cramped metal boxes with pumps attached to their utters and this tears at the heart of the scarecrow.

When he finally travels home for the day on the train, the scarecrow sees a sign being fastened together advertising the food produced by the factory. The scarecrow's face is right there on the sign for everyone to see.

Again, the scarecrow is saddened by what he sees that he has been a part of. But like a lot of heroes in good stories, the scarecrow decides he will not accept the false image of the factory food. He returns home to his modest little farm and gathers up his precious, organic crops and drives back into the city in his truck...What?! You didn't know scarecrows drive trucks?!

The scarecrow sets up a food stand in the city and offers meals to the public made with verified all-natural ingredients. The scene ends moving out and away from his little eatery and a sign that says, 'Cultivate a Better World'.

Chipotle is not directly mentioned in the film. However, there are a few subtleties alluding to their part in the film which are done in very creative ways.

So, how has Chipotle raised the bar with this brilliant film? They told a story about how it is difficult in this day and age to trust exactly what is in our food and how it is made. They have taken a stand and told us that compromising on the food they serve us is not in line with the story they are attempting to tell to their customers.

After watching the film, I wondered what kind of food quality other restaurants are serving. It was not difficult to think of several that are telling a revolting story through the food they sell.

Even now as I write this, I find myself craving the naturally superior food that Chipotle serves. I want to be a part of that story because Chipotle is telling a remarkable story. I feel safe taking my kids there because I know they will take care of our health by not violating it with chemically altered food.

The scarecrow film could have backfired and caused a negative reaction with people. However, it quickly went positively viral and put other food-related businesses on notice that the bar had been raised. Chipotle put the question in our minds that we ask ourselves when visiting other restaurants, *"Are they serving me food made from completely natural ingredients?"*

If not, they must not care and therefore must be telling a stupid story.

Chipotle has committed to telling me a meaningful story that they care about me first, and not their corporate coffers.

To watch the scarecrow film and read an amazing interview with Moonbot Studios about the creation of the film, go to the following URL:

http://theweek.com/article/index/249656/interview-the-brilliant-minds-behind-chipotles-haunting-scarecrow-ad

Challenge yourself to commit your business to raise the bar! Get off the fence! Decide now that you and your business are going to tell a remarkable story and raise the bar for every other business in your industry!

Do or do not...*there is no fence!*

2. Who is my Audience?

When producers and directors create a movie, it is not created to appeal to everyone. The story will only matter to a certain demographic of people. An action movie may appeal mostly to men age 18-35 just as a history biopic will appeal to those interested in history.

If you try to create something to appeal to everyone, it will end up appealing to no one. Can you imagine a producer trying to create a movie that appeals to everyone? That movie would be six hours long about a guy who falls in love with a woman back during the French Revolution, but the man is from the future and traveled back in time while being chased by aliens. There will also be a football game in the movie where the underdog is at fourth and goal from the three-yard line with 2.7-seconds left on the game clock.

Oh yeah, and the woman has an animated dog that talks and says the funniest things in a British accent. Did I mention the police chase too?

Do you see what I am getting at? Movie producers do not try to create movies that everyone will love. It is impossible! So why would you want to try and target everyone as your customer? It does not make sense.

It is also very expensive to try and appeal to everyone and gain them as a customer. You would pretty much have to advertise...*everywhere.*

So the question to ask yourself is, "*Who does my company's story matter to the most?*" The answer to that question is your perfect audience.

I read an article on Entrepreneur.com recently that talked about being clear on who your customers are:

You don't know your audience. If you aren't the target customer ... well, who is? Invest the time and money to identify not just who your customers are but how they behave. How do they live and work? Where do they research purchases? Who influences their buying behavior--peers, review sites, Facebook friends? Have a clear and full picture of the individual you are trying to reach, aka your "buyer persona."

The more you can narrow down who your audience is, the easier it is to find them and tell your story to them. This is not a book or even a chapter about how to figure out who exactly your target market is. The best piece of advice I can give is to narrow it down as much as you can. You will want to create what is called an avatar of your perfect customer. That does not mean you are going to draw a picture of your customer as a nine-foot tall, bluish, human-like creature from the movie, *Avatar*. An avatar is just a precise and detailed representation of your perfect customer. Creating one will help you know who you are telling your story to.

As a roofing contractor, I knew exactly who my perfect avatar was, a property manager of condominium homeowner associations. I had it narrowed down even further than that. The property manager had less than desirable dealings with other roofing contractors and was looking for a reliable contractor to service her HOA clients. My perfect property manager also had close dealings with other managers and had great potential for being a referral source.

Anyway, you get the point, right? You need to know who your perfect customer avatar is just like you know who your best friend is. The more you know, the more you will know how to serve them.

Because I got to know my property manager clients, I learned that the one thing that drove them nuts more than anything else was talking to homeowners. It's usually a negative conversation. When a homeowner calls a property manager, it's usually to report bad news like a roof leak, someone parking in their spot, or a neighbor's dog crapping on their lawn. When you deal with those kinds of calls all day, there is only one thing worse than that, getting a second call from a homeowner about the original issue.

Once I learned about that point of pain from my existing clients, it was easy to get new clients by addressing their pain and offering a remedy.

Finding the Anxiety

Most everyone has anxiety of some kind. We all have frustrations, stress, anxiety, despair, anger, sadness, etc. over something. Finding those points of pain in your customers gives you the opportunity to be their hero and most trusted advisor. You can only accomplish that by first knowing exactly who your perfect customer is and then getting to know them personally. You know the kind of pain a friend is experiencing. Find out what that is in your customers.

When I see the property managers I worked with, I am greeted with smiles and hugs. That's the kind of relationship I want you to strive for with your customers.

Get used to hugs!

What do they want?

During my time as an entrepreneur, I have figured out a very important point about what people really want.

People just want to feel good!

It's simple, yes. But it's so very true.

Yes, people want money and cars and houses and boats and love and respect and whiter teeth, but they want all those things because they think it will make them feel good.

What do you really want in your life? What do you want to own? What social status do you hope to achieve? Where do you want to go?

Why do you want to achieve all of that? **Because you want to feel good!**

Your customers have hopes and dreams too. Why? Because they want to feel good!

Think of movies like, *Remember the Titans*, *Forest Gump*, and *The Blind Side*. People watch movies like that because they want to feel good. They see themselves in those stories. They see themselves as the characters...as heroes. Why? Because it makes them feel good.

Your customers want to feel good. They buy from you because they want to see themselves in your story. People bought iPods from Apple because they wanted to be a part of the story Steve Jobs was telling. And people continue to buy products from Apple because they want to be a part of the story Steve continues to tell through the legacy he built and the story he told.

Best-selling author and sales authority, Jeffrey Gitomer, says, "*People don't like to be sold, but they love to buy.*" People buy because they feel good about the story you are telling. Everything your business does tells a story to your customers.

People are pretty smart these days...and a little skittish. They are smart because they have Google and skittish because the economy tanked. They can tell pretty quickly if they are going to have a good experience with your product or not. All they have to do is ask Google or all their friends on Facebook. Yeah, people know if they are going to feel good about your story...usually within seconds.

People are not as loose with their money as they were during the boom years before 2008. Believe it or not, people need good stories more today than they have in a long time. People want to heal from the traumas they experienced. A lot of people lost all their worldly possessions. Many of those people never got them back or recovered enough of their self-respect that they had before things got bad. Being part of a remarkable story gives people hope. Can you give them that story?

I've learned that people will forget what you said, people will forget what you did, but people will never forget how you made them feel.
     -Maya Angelou

People will never forget how your story made them feel and especially how they felt as a part of your story.

You will be learning more about why it is important to know who it is exactly that you want to do business with as we get further into the sections of this book about your marketing systems.

3. **Where is Your Story Going?**

Once you know who your audience is, you have to figure out where you are taking them in your story. When a director is creating a movie, he has to know where he is taking the story. He has to know how the protagonist develops throughout the story. He has to know how to introduce the protagonist to the audience so they will form a bond with that character as they overcome conflicts to get to the triumphant climax at the end of the story.

When you get a new customer, what is the life cycle of that customer in your business? Do they purchase from you and then move on or is there a relationship that has started that will grow over time through their experiences with your business and its story?

I learned a lesson a long time ago from marketing authority, Dan Kennedy, who said, "*You don't get a customer to make a sale; you make a sale to get a customer.*"

This is directly related to the mindset that you have about your customers and the story you are telling them. Trying to get a new customer to make a sale is a short-term strategy for a short-term business. It is like experiencing a story without a hero. In business, there's a term called, *lifetime value of a customer.*

The basic definition of lifetime value is the value in dollars spent by a customer with your company over their lifetime as your customer.

A business focused on getting customers to make sales is a business that has no clue what the lifetime value is of their customers because those customers do not stick around long enough for the business to make the calculation.

When you have the mindset that you are trying to make a sale to get a customer, you have developed the strategy of a long-term business. You could even lose money on the first sale without losing any sleep because you know that you now have a customer that you will build a long-lasting relationship with. You can also afford to lose money or break even on the initial sale because you know the lifetime value of your customers is high.

Business owners with a long-term relationship mindset and who know the lifetime value of their customers have the remarkable story mindset. They know where the story is going and how to serve their customers throughout that story.

When you know where your story is going, you will know how to bring your customers along within it.

In his book, *The Dan Sullivan Question*, author Dan Sullivan, asks the following question:

"If we were having this discussion three years from today, and you were looking back over those three years, what has to have happened in your life, both personally and professionally, for you to be happy with your progress?"

It really is an amazing question and causes you to do some soul-searching-type thinking. Where *is* your business going? If you and I were having a discussion about your business even just 12 months from now, what has to have happened with the story you are currently telling for you to be happy with your progress?

Questions to Answer

1. **Why does your business matter?** If you do not answer that question, your customers will tell you why it doesn't.
2. **Who is your perfect customer?** Remember, you cannot tell your story to everyone so tell it to those who matter to your business.
3. **Where is your story going?** Are you building long-lasting relationships with your customers or letting them go after a quick sale?

Chapter 2

A Short Blurb about Branding

Have you ever considered what your brand is? The average person thinks a brand is just a logo. Your brand *is not* your logo! It is a recognizable part of your brand. Your logo is your brand image. It is what people visually recognize about your company. But your brand is not just your logo.

Your brand *is a story*.

I am a subscriber to marketing thought leader, Seth Godin's blog and Seth sends out his blog posts every day through email. One of his recent posts explains perfectly how your brand is a story:

The Brand is a Story, But it's a Story About You, Not About the Brand

Why prefer Coke over Pepsi or GE over Samsung or Ford over Chevy?

In markets that aren't natural monopolies or where there are clear, agreed-upon metrics, how do we decide?

Yes, every brand has a story—that's how it goes from being a logo and a name to a brand. The story includes expectations and history and promises and social cues and emotions. The story makes us say we "love Google" or "love Harley"... but what do we really love?

We love ourselves.

We love the memory we have of how that brand made us feel once. We love that it reminds us of our mom, or growing up, or our first kiss. We support a charity or a soccer team or a perfume because it gives us a chance to love something about ourselves.

We can't easily explain this, even to ourselves. We can't easily acknowledge the narcissism and the nostalgia that drives so many of the apparently rational decisions we make every day. But that doesn't mean that they're not at work.

More than ever, we express ourselves with what we buy and how we use what we buy. Extensions of our personality, totems of our selves, reminders of who we are or would like to be.

Great marketers don't make stuff. They make meaning.

Seth says it perfectly. Your brand is a story about you and your business. It's a story people remember and take with them. The story is how they experience you.

How do they define your brand story?

Something else to consider about your brand is that no matter how you see and interpret your brand, your customers will always have their very own ways of interpreting it themselves based on their experience with it.

Remember, everyone has their own ways of being and ways of filtering their experiences to create meaning in their lives. Seth Godin also said the following in relation to brand experience:

"For most of what we experience, though, it's our own interpretation of the experience itself that matters, not what a marketer tells us about how this ranks against that."

Yes, you are telling a story with your business and your brand, but your customers will have their own experience of that story and will share it based on the experience they had. All the more reason to tell a remarkable story!

Think Different

Here's to the crazy ones. The misfits. The rebels. The troublemakers. The round pegs in the square holes. The ones who see things differently. They're not fond of rules. And they have no respect for the status quo. You can quote them, disagree with them, glorify or vilify them. About the only thing you can't do is ignore them. Because they change things. They push the human race forward. And while some may see them as the crazy ones, we see genius. Because the people who are crazy enough to think they can change the world, are the ones who do.

    -Apple TV Ad

When you think different, you think like Apple.

In 1997, Apple came out with a new ad slogan that said, *Apple – Think Different.* Isn't that what Apple has always been about? Steve Jobs was maniacal about Apple being different and creating products that were different. It's an idea that Jobs instilled in the beginning and which established the *Think Different* culture at Apple and the cult following of its raving fans.

Think Different told a story about what Apple stood for and invited people to come into that story by thinking different too.

What is it that causes a company like Apple to think different and to make a difference in the world?

If you think about it, Apple never had more of an advantage than any other technology company that manufactured and sold electronic devices. Did Apple have access to more resources than Dell Computer? It's funny really...Dell founder and CEO, Michael Dell once said of Apple back in 1997 after Steve Jobs returned to the company, *"What would I do? I'd shut it down and give the money back to the shareholders."*

Today, Apple is the most valuable company in the world. Dell...isn't, and was recently looking for a buyer.

It's really a level playing field in the market, so what made Apple rise to become the most valuable company in the world?

It's simple! They tell an amazing story.

A Level Playing Field

In 2001, there were several portable MP3 players on the market. So why was Apple able to come in and introduce the iPod and completely dominate the music player market?

Here's why! Apple had the greatest corporate storyteller that ever existed, Steve Jobs.

When Steve Jobs introduced the iPod for the first time in November of 2001, we were still reeling from the effects of September 11th. The U.S and the rest of the world was still licking its wounds and trying to figure out how to overcome such a dreadful tragedy.

So how did Steve do it? He told a remarkable story. He introduced the iPod and said, *"It's like a thousand songs in your pocket."* Immediately you could relate to what he was saying. You could have a thousand of your favorite songs and carry them all in your pocket. You did not have to carry around hundreds of CDs and a CD player. You had one small, simple device with all your music at your disposal and because it was an Apple product, you knew it was different. You knew it had style and you knew it would work.

Jobs did not have to give you a list of bullet points highlighting how the iPod worked and all the nifty features it had. You didn't care! You just knew you wanted one.

And how did the media share the story of this new, remarkable device? It was easy...Steve gave them their headlines...*A Thousand Songs in Your Pocket.*

He topped that performance with the announcement of the iPod Nano. When he first introduced us to the original iPod, Steve Jobs pulled it from the pocket of his jeans. When he introduced the iPod Nano, which means tiny, Steve pulled it from that little pocket right above the front pocket of his jeans. You know, that little pocket that nobody ever uses. Steve gave that pocket a purpose.

When he introduced the MacBook Air laptop computer, he pulled it from a manila envelope. You immediately knew it was thin, light weight, and of course, amazing!

Steve Jobs and his storytelling platform of Apple gave us a device we did not even know we needed...the iPad. Now we cannot live without it.

For almost 40 years Apple has dazzled us with revolutionary products. After his death in October of 2011, Steve Jobs left behind a legacy of amazing storytellers.

Today we have several companies telling amazing stories like Apple...Amazon, BMW, and Disney, etc. Businesses of all sizes can learn from companies like Apple and be different from all the others in their industry. Remember, you have access to the same resources as your competitors. So who's telling the better story...you...*or them?*

Product Stories

I love companies who tell amazing stories with their products. I have already mentioned my love of the Apple story. BMW shares an amazing story of *the ultimate driving machine*. They have built their whole company around that story and invited everyone into it who wants to experience what it's like to drive *the ultimate driving machine*.

The Walt Disney Company has shared the story that, "When *you wish upon a star, makes no difference who you are. Anything your heart desires, will come to you.*"

They sure made a believer out of me!

Walt Disney was not the only guy that could draw cartoons, but he had a vision of telling an amazing story. He decided his characters were not just going to be part of a cartoon, but part of a story...a story that has touched billions of people.

Walt Disney created an amazing product. He created an experience...a story where all your dreams come true.

Your USP

The term, USP, seems like it has been around for like a thousand years. It stands for, *Unique Selling Proposition.*

There are other variations of it too, like *Unique Value Proposition* and *Unique Marketing Proposition.* Business and marketing gurus have been talking about it forever. There's a reason for that. It's important.

What a USP is, is that special uniqueness of your products, services, and every other part of your business. It's the essence that sets you apart from other companies in your industry, especially your direct competitors.

It's what makes you...*different.*

In our society today, more and more people hate being sold to. Just like Jeffrey Gitomer says about sales, "P*eople don't like being sold, but they love to buy.*"

People love to buy because they feel good about your business and the products you sell. They love your story.

So a unique selling proposition is important, but a unique *story* proposition is even better.

Apple has a unique story proposition with all of its products. Every one of them is unique and tells an amazing story. The story is so amazing that people line up outside of stores for days before the product is available.

How can you create a similar story...for *your* story? What is your *Unique Story Proposition*?

Purple Cow

Author and marketing thought ninja, Seth Godin wrote a book in 2002 called, *Purple Cow.*

In his book, Seth talks about how he and his family were driving along a scenic road one day and noticed all the beautiful scenery, including lots of big, black and white cows. After a short time, Seth and his family no longer noticed the cows anymore because that's how it is with black and white cows over and over again...nobody notices them after a short time. But if you were driving along a road like that and saw a purple cow, now that would get your attention!

How often do you see purple cows? A purple cow is interesting. You might even turn your car around and pull off the side of the road to take pictures of it to show your family and friends and post it on Facebook. Seeing a purple cow after all, is a remarkable story.

This is what we deal with every day. We are constantly bombarded with advertising and marketing that is just like all the rest...asking us to do the same thing. It is not until we see a purple cow that we start paying attention...that is until all the cows are purple...but then you see a yellow cow.
People love new and exciting and they love to be a part of these stories. Keep delivering new and exciting content, products, and services and your customers will love you and your story and they will tell everyone they know about the purple cow they saw.

Of course, none of Seth's books ever have interesting titles, do they? If you are not following Seth Godin, you are missing out on some the most genius thoughts, ideas, and manifestos on business and marketing ever. Follow Seth at SethGodin.com

We are Conditioned NOT to be Different

When my daughter was in first grade, I helped out in her classroom one day around Christmas time. That day, the teacher had the students create gingerbread houses.

Instead of gingerbread though, the students used graham crackers. Each student was given four graham crackers and a small, empty milk carton, like the ones kids get at lunchtime in the cafeteria.

The students were given instructions to fasten the graham crackers to all the sides of the milk carton by spreading frosting on the crackers and to then press them onto the milk carton.

Anyone that has ever handled graham crackers knows that just breathing on one will cause it to break into a million pieces.

It didn't take five (5) minutes before there were broken graham crackers all over the classroom...except on the desk of one little boy. On his desk was just one (1) broken cracker. You see, that little guy decided that it would work out much better for the crackers and thus the whole 'gingerbread' house if he spread the frosting on the sides of the milk carton first and then gently pressed the graham cracker over the frosting.

I watched that little boy and saw the making of a genius. No sooner did he bask in his innovative glory than the teacher came stomping over to scold him for not following directions.

Creativity and innovation crushed!

I don't know how long it would typically take blood to boil, but on that day, it took mine about three seconds. I had to summon all of my restraint to not verbally crush that teacher into pulp.

Who knows what happened to that little boy after that day. Actually, I do. I was that little boy. Not literally, but I remember my own similar experiences in school and they robbed me of so many creative opportunities to be my own unique genius.

Today, I see the results of stories like that little boy. So many of us were told to sit still, be quiet, follow directions explicitly, do it like everyone else is doing it, etc. And what are the results? Too many people out there – business owners, trying to do it like everyone else instead of finding their own Unique Story Proposition.

I get it. It's easy to fall into that trap. It's easy to succumb to the thinking that you have to do it like everyone else is doing it or you will be scolded or sent to the principal's office.

Trying to tell the Same Story

Can you imagine if everyone in your community wore the exact same outfit every day and every outfit was brown? How would you differentiate yourself from everyone else who was wearing the same thing you were? It's tough to distinguish a unique story when it looks like everyone is telling the same one.

Businesses do this all the time! They try to tell the same story as other businesses. They are all competing with the same features – They have been in business for "X" many years, they are bonded, they have insurance, you can trust them, their products are guaranteed, they discovered a *new* fruit in the Amazon that cures stupidity that not even the Amazonians know of, and everyone in their building smiles and smells good.

The Three (3) Forbidden Phrases

A friend and associate of mine who goes by the name, Fireman Mike LeMoine, owns a very successful marketing agency in Albuquerque, New Mexico called, Maverick Web Marketing. It helps local businesses dominate their competition with effective marketing strategies.

I recently read a blog article by Fireman Mike that talked about the three (3) forbidden phrases in marketing. Here they are in Fireman Mike's own words:

There are certain phrases that, if used in your advertising, will guarantee that your advertising results will be terrible and yes—I do guarantee that you are using them in your ads right now. But before I tell you what they are, I want you to get the phone book right now and open the phone book up to your ad. If you don't have an ad in the phone book, then get your brochure, your newspaper ad, your website, or any other advertisement or marketing piece that you use, because I'm going to give you 3 evaluations in just a second so you can see if your ad passes or fails.

Okay, so you should have your ad ready now. But before I give you the evaluations, let me ask you some simple, but important questions:

"Do you always feel forced into a price-competitive situation in your industry? Do you feel like your customers only care about price? Are you always cutting your profits so that you can match a competitor's price? If so, pay close attention to what I'm about to show you because I'm about to explain the biggest reason for those problems.

So here's the deal, the 3 Forbidden Phrases that you should never use in advertising are phrases or statements that include platitudes. Now, let me give you the definition of a platitude.

A platitude is defined as "words or phrases that are drearily commonplace and predictable that lack power to evoke interest through overuse or repetition, that nevertheless are stated as though they were original or significant."

These are words and phrases like: highest quality, biggest selection, largest inventory, best service, been in business since 1776 BC, family owned, gets the job done right the first time, fast, residential and commercial, free estimates, locally owned and operated, #1 in satisfaction, we're better, why pay more, lowest prices, we care, conveniently located, professional, experienced, affordable, board certified, accredited, we're different, advanced techniques, call today, dependable, etc. Do you get the point yet?

Now look, I'm not saying that you shouldn't actually be these kinds of things, but I am saying that they are all platitudes. Every one of those statements and phrases are drearily commonplace and predictable, they lack power to evoke interest through overuse or repetition, and they were nevertheless stated as though they were original or significant. They're all platitudes, my friend. And, I'm going to make you two guarantees about these platitudes right now. The first guarantee is this:

Guarantee #1 *– I guarantee you are using platitudes just like these in all of your advertisements right now—especially if you advertise in the Yellow Pages. Here in Albuquerque, I've looked through all of these books myself and there is not one ad yet that passes the 3 evaluations I'm about to give you.*

Guarantee #2 – *The second guarantee is this—using these platitudes in your advertisements has made your advertising results dismal for as long as you've used them. This means you've left an untold sum of money on the table—money that you could have had in your bank account already if you would have applied the principles I'm about to teach you.*

Now, I understand that you may have been running ads like this for 10, 20, or 30 years—even longer than that—and have been getting what most people would consider pretty good results that whole time.

But what if I could show you that you could have got even better results? It's true—better results are possible and even inevitable when you eliminate platitudes. And by everybody, I mean everybody, including you and your competitors use platitudes in your advertising and marketing.

What this means is that there is a huge market opportunity for the first company in your industry to fix this problem. I'll explain more about fixing this problem in just a second, but first let me give you the 3 evaluations. Okay, are you ready? Here we go...

Platitude Evaluation #1 – Well I would hope so.

I want you to take a look at any claim you've made in your ad and ask yourself if a customer or prospect could or would, automatically respond with the statement, "Well I would hope so." For example here's a line from an ad for a plumber that says "Plumbing Service and Repair." Well I would hope so, you are a plumber right?

Another one says they are "licensed, bonded and insured," and that they "fix faucets and fixtures, water heaters, tubs and showers, etc." Well I would hope so. You're a plumber. What else would you do? I mean, it's so painfully obvious that it's ridiculous.

Or how about an ad that says, "committed to honest, ethical service." Well I would hope so! What else would you expect them to say? Hey we're lousy, we'll show up late, make your house dirty, expose our backsides to your wife and kids, and make sure that the problem that we fixed will break again a few weeks after we fix it. Of course not! Everybody is going to say great things about themselves if they can get away with it.

So what about your ad? How did you do? Do you have any of these painfully obvious statements that would cause someone to say, "Well I would hope so"? Be honest with yourself and check. Okay, on to the second evaluation:

Platitude Evaluation #2 – Who else can say that?

Pay close attention to this one, because the question is not who else can do what you do, but who else can say what you say. The answer is usually anyone and everyone.

A painter in Idaho says that he's "Idaho's best." Who else can say that? Now this guy might actually be the best in Idaho and the best in the entire universe for all I know, but do you actually believe it just because he said it? Who else can say that? Can't the guy on the next page who says "where integrity and quality meet" also say that he's Idaho's best? Of course he can. Or a painter who says, "every job is a work of art." Who else can say that? Again, anybody and everybody can say it. That's who.

See, these statements are drearily predictable and commonplace and they lack power to evoke interest. And you know what, they were nevertheless stated as though they were original or significant. Now look at your ad. Read a few lines and then ask yourself this, "Who else can say that?" If one of your competitors can say it, you failed this evaluation.

One of the most common platitudes here is to tell us how long you've been in business. Everybody thinks it matters, but I promise you it doesn't. Here's an illustration—how about this, a Chiropractor who thinks you should visit his practice because he's been a Chiropractor for over 29 years. Who else can say that? Well, how about the competitor who has been serving for over 30 years. See what I mean?

To take this one step further, let's move on to the last evaluation, which might hurt the most...

Platitude Evaluation #3 – The Cross Out/Write-In Test

For this evaluation, I'm going to have you cross out the name of your company in your advertisement and then write in the name of your competitor. Now tell me this, is the ad still valid? If so, you've just failed the test. For example, I looked at an attorney's ad for Roberts Law Office. I crossed out Roberts Law Office and put in Jones and Johnson Law. The ad is still valid. These attorneys have all failed when it comes to marketing their practices. They might all be great or they might be terrible, but I can't tell from their ads—it looks to me like they're all the same.

Or how about an auto repair shop, Buster's Auto Repair, where they offer Honest, Quality repair and they have the latest technology and diagnostic equipment. Then they have a laundry list of services that they offer and an incredible 24,000 miles or 24 month warranty. Amazing! But right next to this ad is Champion Automotive who says that they'll "take care of you," and they include their own laundry list of services that is nearly identical to the one we just saw, but get this—they have a 25 month, 25,000 mile warranty.

Do you all get it? These ads all fail. Even though their warranties differ by 1 month and 1,000 miles, they are still basically the same so they don't pass the cross out/write in test. I can give you hundreds of other examples in these phone books for insurance companies who can give you "fast easy quotes" or dentists who offer "complete dental care" or landscape contractors who "cut to perfection," but the bottom line is that none of these ads pass the cross out/write-in test or the other platitude evaluations.

What about you? Cross out your company name in your ad and write in the name of your closest competitor. Go ahead and do it right now. Now tell me, is the ad still valid? I mean really. I don't care if you absolutely know that you have higher quality than your competitor because your competitor can still say that they have higher quality than you even if it's not true. Another way to illustrate this is to do it in reverse. Cross out your competitors name on their ad and write your name in there. See, the ad is still valid, isn't it? Bad news, my friend, you failed the test.

These 3 evaluations come straight out of marketing guru Rich Harshaws groundbreaking book, Monopolize Your Marketplace.

You see, platitudes cause your marketplace to assume that you and your competitors are all the same. That might not be true. You might have the best business of its kind in your industry, but since your ads and your competitor's ads all use platitudes, then the marketplace can't tell who actually offers the best value, so they call you up and ask you the same question that you're probably really sick of hearing, *which is "How much do you charge?" My friend, it doesn't have to be that way.*

Not only does Fireman Mike LeMoine own and run Maverick Web Marketing, he's also a full-time fireman and paramedic in Albuquerque. Mike is telling an amazing story in so many ways!

So let's test out what Fireman Mike just showed you. Open up a Yellow Pages book (if you even have one) to any contractor section like electricians, plumbers, roofers, etc. and see if any of the ads stand out from the others.

Can you see the three platitudes being used in the ads? Do you notice any ads that adhere to the statement: *Well I would hope so?*

Do you see any ads that make promises like, 24-hour service, licensed & bonded, or satisfaction guaranteed? *Who else can say that?*

Are there ads where you can cross out the name of the business and replace it with the business from another ad? Does the ad still look relevant? If so, it failed the *cross-out/write-in test.*

Now do the same exercise with your own ads and marketing. I ran some of my old advertising and marketing through the three (3) platitude filters and was shocked at what I saw. You may want to do that exercise near the bathroom. What you discover might make you sick.

The definition of insanity has been described as doing the same thing over and over again expecting a different result. Doing the same advertising and marketing as everyone else in your industry and expecting to be different is ten (10) kinds of insane.

It is total insanity and yet it happens far too often. But it doesn't have to be that way. One by one, business owners can choose something different. You can choose to *be* different, to act different, and to tell a different story.

It's time for you to *think different* and to find your own purple cow! Make your business and your story so interesting that people will stop to take notice!

Share a remarkable story!

Brand Consistency

Recently, I read the book, *The Slight Edge*, by Jeff Olson. The main principle in the book is that even the smallest, little things done consistently every day will have a compounding affect later on.

The compounding affect is best illustrated by a story Jeff shares in his book:

The Water Hyacinth

The water hyacinth is a beautiful, delicate-looking little plant. Prized as an ornament, it sports six-petal flowers ranging from a lovely purplish blue, to lavender, to pink. You can find it floating on the surface of ponds in warm climates around the word.

The water hyacinth is also one of the most productive plants on earth; its reproductive rate astonishes botanists and ecologists. Although a single plant can produce as many as 5,000 seeds, the method it prefers for colonizing a new area is to grow by doubling itself, sending out short runner stems that become 'daughter plants'.

If a pond's surface is fairly still and undisturbed, the water hyacinth may cover the entire pond in thirty days.

On the first day, you won't even notice it. In fact, for the first few weeks you will have to search very hard to find it. On day 15, it will cover perhaps a single square foot of the pond's surface...a barely significant dollop of color dotting the expanse of placid green.

On the twentieth day (two-thirds of the way to the end of the month), you may happen to notice a dense little patch of floating foliage, about the size of a small mattress. You would be easily forgiven if you mistook it for a boy's inflatable life raft, left behind during a family picnic.

On day 29, one-half of the pond's surface will be open water.

On the thirtieth day, the entire pond will be covered by a blanket of water hyacinth.

You will not see any water at all.

Consistency is doing something every day that adds to your story. It may be the slightest improvement or adjustment that goes unnoticed. But over time, those little improvements will add up to the most amazing story and one your customers will be excited to be a part of.

Five (5) Questions to Answer to Consistently Improve Your Story

1. How can I improve my products and services?

2. What can I add to them to increase the value to my customers?

3. How can I improve the way I serve my customers?

4. How can I add to their experience as part of my company's story?

5. How can my company's story improve the story of my customer?

The most powerful way to improve your story is to ask your customers. People like to give their opinions and especially like it when their opinions cause a change. It makes them feel important.

Since your story is all about your customers, why not ask them how you can make it better. By consistently surveying your customers, you can create a story and experience what will keep them coming back.

"My pleasure!"

When I was a kid my Dad would take me to Chick-Fil-A whenever we went to the local mall, which was not frequent. They had the best chicken nuggets!

What I noticed not too long ago is that Chick-Fil-A tells a great story. Their food is excellent, the service is great, and they are closed on Sundays so their employees can be with their loved ones and enjoy a day of rest.

Another part of the amazing story at Chick-Fil-A is that their story is consistent at every one of their restaurants. I can expect the same quality food, the same service...and when I say thank you, I can expect my server to respond with, "M*y pleasure!*".

Chick-Fil-A tells a story that says it's a pleasure to know you, feed you, and serve you...except on Sundays. Perfect cohesion every time!

Is your story consistent?

Is the experience your customers have consistent to their last experience? Are they treated with the same attention to detail? Are they given the same level of service each and every time? Do they get the same level of satisfaction with your products as before?

Whether their experience is amazing or it totally sucks, your customers will have a certain expectation each time they engage your business. And the pressure is on especially if you are providing an amazing experience. They will want *and* expect it every time.

One thing is for certain, if you are sharing a remarkable story with your customers and providing a great experience, they will expect it the next time and every time thereafter. Until they don't get it, of course! But you won't let that happen, because you are committed.

Keep your story consistent across the entire customer experience. Keep it consistent in your advertising, marketing, and your ever-evolving brand and story creation.

Chapter 3

Positioning Your Story

You cannot go anywhere in the civilized world without seeing major brands positioning themselves to be seen by customers and potential customers. It's both advertising and marketing in one. The companies have positioned their stories to draw in new customers and keep the conversation going and stay top-of-mind with existing ones.

When a major publisher puts out a new book they hope will become a best seller, they position that book to be found by as many potential readers as possible. That means, placing the book in all the major book retailers, like Barnes & Noble and Amazon. The publisher may also use social media platforms like Facebook, Twitter, and YouTube to position the book for maximum exposure. They may take out ads in traditional advertising media like TV commercials, print ads, and online ads.

When a major publisher puts out a new book they hope will become a best seller, they position that book to be found by as many potential readers as possible. That means, placing the book in all the major book retailers, like Barnes & Noble and Amazon. The publisher may also use social media platforms like Facebook, Twitter, and YouTube to position the book for maximum exposure. They may take out ads in traditional advertising media like TV commercials, print ads, and online ads.

Positioning My Story

When I started my roofing company, I knew I needed to position my company and story in front of my target market, which were condominium homeowner association management companies.

Luckily for me, all the management companies belonged to a national organization, called Community Associations Institute (CAI). CAI held monthly luncheons that were attended by managers, HOA board members, and vendors like me. CAI also has an online directory of all its members. Twice a year they also have a trade expo.

By joining CAI, I positioned my company in front of the people that would become my clients. I networked with them, visited their offices, and educated them on the value of using a company like mine for their roofing needs.

It paid off big time and I have enjoyed great relationships with my clients ever since.

Storytelling Platforms

Apple

Yes, I've mentioned Apple a few times in this book. I may even mention them a few more times before it's over. Apple has done a superb job at not only telling an amazing story, but also positioning their story to be heard and experienced by millions of people.

Creative advertising and marketing is a big part of their success, but Apple has done something else that has really catapulted them to masters of the technology universe...they created a *platform*.

When Apple announced the new iPhone in January 2007, I knew I was watching the dawning of a new age. I don't know what it was like for people seeing photos of Earth for the first time or watching Neil Armstrong walk on the moon, but when I first saw the iPhone, I was spellbound!

I remember when I bought my first iPhone. I felt like I had just joined an exclusive club. When I saw others with their iPhones, it seemed like we were old friends. Now it seems like everyone has an iPhone and so the mystique has worn off.

When the first iPhone went on sale, everyone had the same set of pre-installed apps. We could all take photos, send text messages, make phone calls, access the internet, download and listen to music, and watch videos.

When I had my iPhone in my hand for the first time, I knew I was part of a new story. After years of frustration with cell phones and their limited capabilities, I now had a masterpiece of fine technology that was easy to use and performed functions I had only hoped would be available twenty (20) years later.

It was not until the App Store opened that Apple had unleashed the iPhone as a storytelling platform. I remember opening the App Store for the first time and was totally blown away at the over 300 apps available. Looking back, it seems so funny being able to browse all those apps in about an hour. Now, that would almost be impossible to do in a lifetime.

Now, the iPhone is a platform for app creation. New apps come out every day to go along with the over 800,000 apps already available. Apple created an app revolution. Apple's ad says it all: *"There's an app for that."* Our entire world seems to be run by apps now.

Apple has created platforms for almost the entire human experience. They are one of the biggest players in the desktop computer industry. They gave us iTunes and the iPod and a whole new way to experience music with *1000 songs in our pockets.* They gave us a phone, a music player, and internet connectivity device all in one in the iPhone. Then they gave us the device we didn't know we needed...the iPad.

If the rumors are true, we may have our TV experience completely upended with the iTV. It seems that all that's left is for Apple to dominate how we experience smell and food.

Apple created an easily recognizable brand image and they position it well in the marketplace. Their logo of an apple with a bite taken out of it represents a remarkable story. When I see the logo, I'm reminded that I'm different and that it's okay for me to *think different.* The bite taken out of the apple tells me that Apple products and their story is something to be experienced and not just viewed from afar. Apple's logo has undergone various changes over the years to what it has become today. Today, their logo reflects their strict adherence to creative industrial design. For kicks and giggles, do a search online for Apple's original logo. You are sure to notice an incredible difference.

What is perhaps the most amazing part of the Apple story is the share-ability of their products. Their ultimate dominance of positioning is how the products are shared amongst those who own them with those who almost do.

Apple itself is a platform for amazing stories and they have created products and stories around them that have affected the stories we live.

Amazon

When Amazon.com burst onto the internet scene in 1995, founder, Jeff Bezos decided to start out by selling books. Today, Amazon seems to sell everything but the moon.

Just as Apple revolutionized entire industries, Amazon has revolutionized the publishing industry, specifically self-publishing.

Just as Apple brought the music industry to its knees, Amazon is doing the same for traditional publishing. Self-published authors are quickly rising up the ranks of the Amazon best-sellers lists. Fiction author, John Locke, is the first self-published author to sell over one million books on Amazon and he has several number one best sellers along with a rabid fan following.

Amazon created a platform for people to tell stories, literally, and position their stories to be heard.

It used to be nearly impossible to get a big publisher to publish your book. If you have heard the term, *starving actor*, a starving author was even worse.

With a good book and some creative marketing, it is now entirely possible for almost anyone to write a book and even make some money with it.

Aside from the monetary possibilities of self-publishing, Amazon has made it possible for people to share their ideas, their know-how, and the dormant stories they have had inside them waiting to be drawn out. Amazon gives writers a platform for authority. Being an author still has its allure of expertise that people find credible and trustworthy.

Amazon has created the ultimate platform for people to position themselves as authorities in their fields. (More on authority positioning later.)

Facebook

When Tim Berners Lee introduced us to his invention called the World Wide Web in the early 1990s, did he have any idea what it would become?

History will tell for sure, but the internet could go down as the greatest invention of all time.

One thing is for sure, the internet has become the greatest platform for storytelling and sharing...EVER! Our earliest ancestors would certainly fall over from a stroke if transported to our day to see what cave paintings and smoke signals have turned into.

The 800-pound gorilla of storytelling is Facebook. Even founder, Mark Zuckerburg could not have foreseen what Facebook would become or will become as it continues to evolve as the ultimate storytelling and positioning platform.

I use Facebook a lot. I use it mostly on my iPhone and when one of my friends posts something new, a little message tab pops up at the top of my screen letting me know that I have *new stories* available.

That's all Facebook really is – a great, big place to share stories. Stories are shared with text, photos, videos, and links to external web pages.

We collect friends on Facebook. We like and share each other's stories and create a community with each other. We position ourselves as whomever we choose to be, which can change from day to day.

One day we are positioned as just a regular friend; another day we are a political activist. Some days we might be the class clown; other days we are an expert in our field.

Regardless of how we position ourselves on Facebook, we are there telling stories.

Starbucks

Starbucks is a great story and does a fantastic job of positioning its brand to be seen by their target market, coffee drinkers and, coffee drinkers, well, that seems to be just about everyone in the civilized world.

But Starbucks is not trying to win over everyone – just those willing to spend $4+ for a cup of coffee. Starbucks does offer a nice place to relax, drink coffee, tea, and other drinks and even get some work done on your laptop.

Howard Schultz was director of Marketing for the original Starbucks company in 1981. On a buying trip to Milan, Italy, Schultz noticed coffee bars on practically every corner. The quality espresso as well as the setting as a meeting and social gathering place especially impressed him.

Upon his return to the U.S, Schultz persuaded the owners of Starbucks to introduce espresso at their shops along with the roasted coffee they were selling. The owners agreed to a pilot program of Schultz's. Even after a successful run of the café concept, the Starbucks owners refused to roll it out company wide.

Howard Schultz started his own coffee shop in 1985 and two (2) years later, bought Starbucks from the original owners for $3.8 million. Expansion of the company happened quickly, but without any of the Starbucks shops losing their small company appeal.

It seems everywhere you go there is a Starbucks waiting for you. Starbucks has positioned itself to be found when people want coffee. It has a very recognizable brand image in its logo. And just when you think Starbucks could not possibly build a store anywhere else in the world, they gladly say, "*Here's a place!*"

In Tukwila, Washington, there is a Starbucks that occupies four reclaimed shipping containers...two on the bottom; two on the top.

What about local businesses?

Can local businesses like flower shops, car repair, dentists, landscapers, etc. learn the art of positioning from the big guys?

Of course they can!

In the South Bay beach cities area of Southern California where I grew up, there is a landscaping company that completely dominates the landscaping market.

Finley's Tree and Land Care, Inc. is a family-owned company started in 1975 by, Mike Finley. It wasn't until Mike's sons, Steve and Scott, joined the family business that things really took off.

Along with creating a new brand image, the Finley's positioned themselves perfectly. Their branding can be seen all over their service area. You cannot drive around anywhere without seeing one of their trucks or a crew of guys working at several locations in town.

You can see their brand on billboards, local print advertising, and t-shirts. They sponsor local sports teams and host local events, including ping-pong and horseshoe tournaments.

The Finley's do not have more access to advertising and marketing resources than other landscaping companies. Their workers are not necessarily more gifted than the other companies. But the Finley's know how to position themselves better than the other guys. You can see their story everywhere.

When someone thinks about landscaping in the South Bay, more often than not, they think of Finley's first.

You Cannot be Everywhere

Let's face it, you cannot possibly position your story to be seen and heard everywhere all the time. It's about being found when people are looking. Trying to be everywhere all the time is stalking and highly frowned upon in most countries.

Previously, you learned about being clear on who your customers are. To position your story, you also need to know where they are, where they go, and when and why they will be there.

Sometimes it's hard to position your business so people will notice because, let's face it, people are busy, distracted, and annoyed with being busy and distracted.

It is difficult not to roll my eyes when I see disruptive ads in places where people are not going to pay attention to them. Most advertising is disruptive push-type advertising where companies try and *push* their products at you rather than pull or attract you to them.

Remember, marketing is a continual conversation you have with your customers. You want to position your story in a way that invites them to become a part of that conversation.

You also want to find out where conversations are already taking place where you can plug in your story.

Appropriate Positioning

In order to attract more of your perfect customers, your business needs perfect positioning, which means positioning your brand where your customers will see it. In the early 1960s, a man named, Bob Byers built and opened a water park located off of interstate 15 in the Mojave Desert of Central California.

Originally called, Lake Delores, after Bob's wife, the park was built as a play place for Bob's extended family, it was soon opened to the public with the idea that people who were traveling in the middle of nowhere between Los Angeles and Las Vegas might want to stop and zoom down steel watersides.

The park actually lasted ten (10) years before interest waned, forcing the park to close.

Lake Delores changed hands several times over the next twenty five (25) years, with each new owner seeing a new 'vision' of how a water park in the middle of the desert would attract people from all over.

People may come to a baseball field in the middle of an Iowa cornfield, but not a water park in who-knows-where California.

My family and I stopped at Lake Delores once on a pit stop along our annual family vacation. It was most likely just to satisfy my dad's thirst for all things novel and different. I still remember the blister on my leg from sliding down a metal water slide with too little water in it. Driving the rest of the way to Las Vegas with a blister on your leg while wearing shorts in a car with vinyl seats just plain sucks!

For a lot of businesses these days, it doesn't make much sense to advertise in the Yellow Pages or the local newspaper. For businesses that sell to the senior market, it makes perfect sense because the older generation still gets most of their news and information from newspapers and they still look for a plumber in the Yellow Pages.

A Thought about the Yellow Pages

What if I told you I knew of a place where you could advertise your business right alongside all of your competitors, would that excite you? And what if I told you that you could have a great big colorful ad with all of your company information right there on the ad?

But wait...there's more.

All you have to do to have this amazing ad is pay hundreds or even thousands of dollars every month while your ad is locked into its position for a whole year.

Isn't that exciting? You could have a super duper ad all year long right next to all of your competitors' ads.

Well, if that doesn't excite you, then you may want to rethink advertising in the Yellow Pages because that's exactly what you will get.

Again, Yellow Pages makes sense for some businesses, but not for most of them. I talk more about the Yellow Pages and similar types of positioning later on this book.

Community-based vs. Commodity-based Positioning

In another blog article by Seth Godin, he talks about the difference between a community-based business and a commodity-based business:

Community-based businesses tell stories. They create remarkable products. They sync up their tribe. They happily surrender market share to the commodity seller--if it's a lower price you want, good luck to you! The community business says, "People like us shop at a place like this." This is where brands live, and where work that matters gets done.

Commodity-based businesses are the ones advertising in the Yellow Pages. They sit there should-to-shoulder with their competitors visually numbing us with platitude-infested ads, which do nothing but force the businesses to compete on price.

And let me be perfectly bold and honest with you, businesses competing on price are telling forgettable stories. Yes, it does feel good to buy something at a reasonable price. We all like getting a discount here and there, but leaving a legacy as the low-price leader in your industry is not a meaningful story. How many elderly people do you know that tell stories to their grandkids about Walmart?

Community-based businesses on the other hand, do exactly what Seth Godin says, *"They tell stories. Meaningful ones! They don't compete on price. They have created an experience for their customers that matter – experiences that are clickable, likeable, and shareable."*

Community-based businesses are those grassroots businesses that are out there active in your community. They are anchored in the community and strategically positioned to be seen and sought. They are in touch with what is going on. They know their customers because their customers are family.

Community-based businesses may be in the Yellow Pages too, but only if their prospective customers go there to look for them. But because all the commodity-based business ads are the same, the community-based ad pops out of the page.

Any business can choose to position themselves as a community-based business by choosing to tell a different story. They can release themselves of the anxiety of competing on price and tell a remarkable story...one where grandpa will say, "A *plumber? Let me tell you about a plumber!*"

Being Found vs. Being Sought

I love what Seth Godin said in one of his blog articles:

"There are proven strategies that generic products can use so that they are more likely to be stumbled upon by someone searching. Name your new book with all sorts of keywords in the title, for example, so it organically ranks higher for those very keywords...

The alternative is to create a product that earns a reputation sufficient that people choose to talk about it, choose to argue about it, choose to look for it. Not something like it, but it!

Nice to be found! Essential to be sought!

This was always a good idea, but in a post-search era of mobile and social, it's now the best idea."

Businesses can no longer afford to hope people will just stumble upon them by some random chance Google search or local drive-by.

Today, your business must be sought after. Your customers must be sharing your story enough that their friends seek you out. Your story must be meaningful enough that it has deep meaning within the mind of your customers.

Flyfishing and Positioning...Waiting vs. Wading

One of my favorite pastimes is fishing. I was destined to love fishing. I grew up bait fishing in the ocean around Southern California and in the lakes and streams of the Rocky Mountains in the Western United States.

My Dad always had a boat docked in the local harbor. I spent a lot of time as a kid on that boat, catching halibut, barracuda, yellowtail, and even some sharks.

During the summers, my family would always take a month-long vacation through Utah, Idaho, Wyoming, and other states around the Rockies. My Dad and I did a lot of trout fishing on those trips. I became quite proficient at catching trout with fresh worms.

It was not until I was fifteen (15) years old that I had an entirely new world of fishing opened up to me. During our usual summer vacation that year, my Dad had lined up two (2) guided river trips for him and me so I could learn flyfishing. Flyfishing is fishing using an artificial fly on the end of the flyfishing line that is attached to the fly rod and reel. I was immediately addicted. It was the greatest way to learn the art of flyfishing. We had an expert river guide on our boat and lots of wide open space on the river, which is great when you are learning flyfishing because it's easy to get your fly caught in trees, bushes, or even people.

Over the years since then, I have caught a ton of trout with my fly rod. One thing I have learned over that time is there is a big difference between regular bait fishing and flyfishing.

With bait fishing, I would attach a worm to a hook and cast it into whatever body of water I was fishing in, lake or stream. Then I would wait for the fish, assuming there were fish nearby, to come and take the bait. There are different tactics to use when bait fishing that can better your chances of finding and catching fish, but it's still a waiting game.

When I am flyfishing, I'm *wading* in the stream, going where the fish are. In a stream, there are various places where I can almost guarantee fish are *waiting* for me. I tie a fly onto my line and drift it over the fish, attracting them to the fly, and POW...a giant trout on my line. During the fall in any free-flowing mountain stream west of the Rockies, I can almost guarantee that I will catch trout. I have learned to *wade* and go where the fish are, instead of *waiting* for them to come to me.

This fishing story applies to businesses. You can create a website, put out some ads, and even create a Facebook page, and wait for people to come to you. Or, you can go where the people are and attract them with your story.

When I am flyfishing, I position myself where the fish are. I take my fly to them. I attract them with a fly that is appealing to them in their particular location.

When you are positioning your brand, position it where your prospects and customers are. If you are telling a remarkable story, in places where they are hanging out, you are sure to get bites and maybe even a giant *trout*.

One thing about flyfishing, though, is you have to approach the fish in a way that will not scare them off. If I am wearing bright colors, waving my arms, screaming, or splashing loudly in the stream, the trout will swim away and I will have to find them elsewhere.

You can just as easily scare off your customers by telling a stupid story. Terrible products and customer service are sure to do that. Do not present that kind of *fly* to them. Give them a *fly*, or a story, that is appealing and attractive and watch them *bite* like crazy.

Reeling it in vs. Playing it

When you are out fishing using bait like worms and a fish swallows the worm, you have to reel in the fish. It takes a little finesse, but it's pretty straightforward, just reel in the fish.

With flyfishing on the other hand, it takes a lot more finesse and requires you to *play* the fish into your net. It's a much more delicate process.

With bait fishing, the fish swallows the bait. With flyfishing, the fish bites at the fly, but then the flyfisherman has to *set* the hook, by giving a gentle, but firm, tug on the fly line to set the hook in the fish's mouth.

Once you have a fish on the fly, the line has to remain tight and upright, forcing the fish's mouth upward. Most of the time, the fish attempt to swim away and free themselves, so you have to let out some line while still keeping it tight and the tip of the fly rod pointed up. By pointing the fly rod up, you keep the fish's mouth pointed up, which keeps the fly snug in its lip.

Once the fish has taken the extra slack out of the line, the fisherman can begin to reel in the fish, while continuing the two actions described above. The fish still may pull some line out, but gradually the fish tires out and it can be reeled all the way into your net.

Playing a fish on the end of a fly line is like the relationship you have with your customers. After you have positioned your story and attracted customers to it, you have to *play* them into your *net*. Sometimes they may resist or pull a little. You just give them a little slack, but you don't let go. Keep your *line* tight and don't let them forget why you have them hooked. Always remind them of the remarkable story you are telling them and their part in that story.

Chapter 4

Telling the Right Story for the Platform

"Play within the reality of the marketplace"
- Gary Vaynerchuck

Things change!

All the time!

And today, things change faster than ever!

As Ferris Beuller said, *"Life moves pretty fast. If you don't stop and look around once in a while, you could miss it."*

Although that quote is true, sometimes it seems impossible to miss anything with all the social media platforms we have these days. A year from now, we will probably have a hundred more. Less than ten (10) years ago we did not have Facebook, Twitter, YouTube, LinkedIn, Pinterest, Instagram, SnapChat, or Farmville. Birds were not angry either.

Each social media platform has its own culture, or ways we communicate within the platform.

On Facebook, we post status updates. On Twitter, we Tweet. On Pinterest we Pin. On YouTube, we broadcast.

Because of the differences in social culture, you have to learn to tell your story appropriate to the platform and the people in it.

Gary Vaynerchuck is a brilliant entrepreneur, marketing thought leader, and author. He wrote a book called, *Jab, Jab, Jab, Right Hook – How to Tell Your Story in a Noisy Social World.*

Gary is a master marketer and has said some brilliant things regarding marketing and social media. Here are some points of wisdom from Gary Vaynerchcuk:

"You have to learn to tell stories on every platform."

As I mentioned above, each social media platform has its own culture and best practices for communication within the platform.

On Twitter, you get one hundred forty (140) characters in your Tweet to tell your story. On Facebook, you better keep your story short too or you will put us to sleep. On Pinterest, you tell your story with images. On SnapChat, you have less than ten (10) seconds to share your story before your photo or video is gone.

No matter what you do, it is your job to tell your story, what your value proposition is along the point of purchase.

Your story **is** your value proposition. It communicates the value that you have and the value that the customer can expect from your business.

And it is *your* job to always be telling your story and to make sure your whole company is telling it too, before, during, and after every transaction.

You have to respect and understand the psychology of why someone is on Pinterest vs. Facebook.

This is part of telling stories appropriate to the platform. But you also have to understand why someone is choosing to consume stories on one platform versus another.

An entire book could be written, and I am sure there is, about the psychology of social media behavior.

White Noise

Are you old enough to remember white noise? I remember it first, as the TV from the movie Poltergeist that sucked the creepy little girl in. It's like the space between channels where the screen is fragmented into millions of white specks jumping all around the screen and a noise that sounds like you are gargling spit in the back of your throat. Who would have thought TV white noise would be so terrifying?

The thing with white noise is it does not get your attention other than causing you to change the channel.

So many businesses try to keep the conversation going with their customers by communicating with white noise. It just makes people want to change the channel.

Just like telling stories appropriate to the platform, you have to find the ways that your customers want to be communicated with. Trying to get your message across on a billboard is white noise when most drivers still text and drive even though it's illegal. They are not looking!
Traditional advertisers are freaking out wondering how to get more eyeballs glued to their messages because people are recording all their TV shows now and fast-forwarding through the commercials. So what have the advertisers done? They have put the commercials in the streaming videos that people are watching online. I usually get on my phone and check out Facebook until the commercials are over. I'm not the only one either.

We cannot create more time, which means we still have a maximum of twenty four (24) hours of attention to give every day, and a third of that attention is spent looking at the backs of our eyelids.

A great battle is going on all the time, a battle for our attention. But even with this battle raging on all the time, we are still suckers for stories. We will still consume stories. Why do we want to fast-forward or redirect our attention until our shows come back on? Because we want to get right back to the stories!

You want the attention of your customers! Quit pushing noise at them! Get back to telling your story and then keep telling it! Give them what they want! Make them feel good! Make them feel part of something meaningful!

Creating Storytellers

There is no better way to position your story than through word-of-mouth marketing. Word-of-mouth marketing is when your customers do your marketing for you. It is where you have turned them into storytellers that share your story with the people they know.

When you create storytellers from your customers they take your story with them. They tell your story when you have affected theirs.

You can train your customers to become storytellers and have them ready to share your story when triggered by words in conversations that remind them of the experience they had with your business.

4 Ways to Turn Customers into Storytellers

1. Remind them of their story and experience with your business and its products – When your customers have a meaningful experience with your business, remind them of it. I do not mean that the next time they come in you should say, *"Remember the great experience you had the last time you were here?"*

Remind them of their great experiences by striving to give them more each time. Make the experience more meaningful by adding to the last one. Give them a better story at each interaction and transaction and they will become powerful storytellers.

2. Reward them – Rewards programs can work really well if properly executed. Rewarding your customers for certain actions, especially their loyalty, can work wonders for your business. Games also work in conjunction with rewards programs. Check out the book, Gamification By Design, by Gabe Zicherman and Christopher Cunningham. The book is focused on web and mobile apps, but you will get plenty of ideas on how to create *gamifcation* into your marketing.

There are tons of books and courses on creating rewards programs and games for your marketing. Find one or two that fit to your marketing strategy and run with it.

3. Turn them into heroes – This may be the one that makes the best storytellers. People love recognition and praise. It's part of our basic human need to love and be loved. When we post our life events on places like Facebook and Twitter, we love the recognition we get from our friends. We feel connected.

There may be no more powerful way to market your business than to turn your customers into the heroes of your story.

4. Success stories – Documenting and sharing the success stories of your customers and their experiences with your products and services, is a powerful way to attract more customers. When people receive special recognition, they want to share it with their friends.

People like Anthony Robins do this very well. I just recently watched a video of one of Anthony's seminars that featured a former U.S Marine on stage. This marine had been in combat five (5) times and deployed about eight (8) times. That's a lot to ask of any soldier. He was suffering from various conditions like post-traumatic stress disorder and other things related to combat service.

This brave veteran was dealing with demons that seemed far worse to him than the conditions of the battlefields he had been in. With Robins' help, he was able to start dealing with those issues head on, just like a marine would do. He made some miraculous progress and was featured on some popular news outlets along with Anthony Robins.

It's a touching story and by featuring the marine on stage, Anthony Robins turned him into a different kind of hero and an amazing success story.

Another person that creates and uses customer success stories extremely well is Mike Koenigs, creator of Traffic Geyser and other excellent marketing tools.

Mike and his team have created some of the best marketing tools on the planet for both online and offline marketing. Every time they launch a new tool or training course to teach the practical and effective use of the tools, Mike puts together a showcase of heroes that have been creative and successful with his tools and training.

Many of those heroes have created large and loyal followings just from being recognized as a Traffic Geyser hero.

Section 2

The Fortune is in the Funnel

Telling a remarkable story is crucial to the success of your business. Building a system for telling your story will make the growth of your business a whole lot easier.

The system for telling your story is called your *marketing funnel*. The term, marketing funnel, has been around for a while and has mostly been used in the online marketing space to describe the system for capturing prospects, promoting marketing content and products, and converting those prospects into customers, and turning customers into longtime followers and loyal fans.

It is a simple concept, however, I am going to show you how this simple concept works in powerful ways to introduce people to your story, get them hooked, and keep them coming back for more. I will show you how your story takes place inside your marketing funnel and how creating an automated marketing system within your funnel will grow your business and increase your profits more than any other activity in your company.

Let's get to it!

On the next page is a simple drawing of your marketing funnel:

The Marketing Funnel

Funnel image 1

As you can see, it is a simple image of a powerful concept. Prospects enter the top of the funnel and progress deeper into the funnel as you engage with them and offer them greater value and opportunities to buy.

Now let's see how your story is told within your marketing funnel.

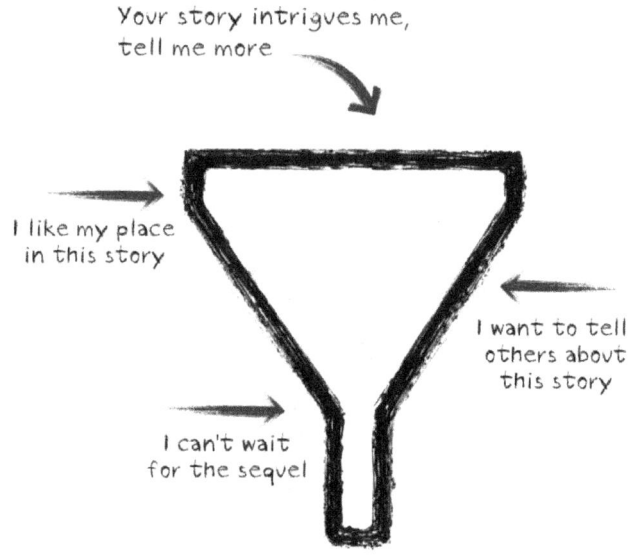

Funnel image 2

Your story intrigues me...Tell me more
Funnel Image 2

At the top of the funnel is where new leads and prospects come in because your story has intrigued them to the point where they want to sample some portion of it.

At this point the prospect is willing to give you their contact info like their email address or phone number in exchange for something from your business. This may be in the form of information like a free report. An example for a chiropractor might be a free report with seven tips on how to heal back pain or a painting contractor offering tips on selecting the right paint for your home.

Whatever it is you give to your prospect in exchange for their info, by doing so, you will be given a way to follow up with them and invite them into the next level of your marketing funnel.

As in the chiropractor or painting contractor example, the next level in the funnel might be setting up an appointment with the prospect or giving them more information like a few short videos.

We will discuss the value of creating compelling content later in the book.

I'd like to experience this story!
Funnel Example #2

Now your prospect has moved down a level in your funnel by giving you their contact info. They have reached the point where they would like to experience your story and how your story can change their life.

This is the point where your prospect is ready to spend some money with you and move from prospect to customer. They believe that what you have to offer them will make them feel good. Remember, that is all anybody ever wants, to feel good.

I love my place in this story...I want to tell others about it!
Funnel Example #2

As your new customer moves deeper into your marketing funnel, they are ready for a richer, more pleasurable experience with your story and are ready and willing to spend more money with you.

Your new customer is ready to share their experience with others, whether face-to-face, over the phone, or on their social media platforms, etc.

This is the point where the customer is willing to give referrals, the ultimate form of appreciation. This is also the point where you *should* be asking for referrals. You should already have a referral generating strategy for this point in the funnel.

We will talk about referrals later when we get into the details of your funnel as your marketing system.

I can't wait for the sequel!
Funnel Example #2

At this level of the funnel, your customer is a raving fan. You have told them a remarkable story and they love their place in that story.

They actively give referrals and share their experience with others. They have purchased from you several times and will continue to do so.

So, we have talked about how your story is told through your marketing funnel. Now let's talk about how your marketing funnel is your marketing system and how it works.

Chapter 5

Your Marketing Funnel System

You now know how your story is told within your marketing funnel, now let's get into how your funnel works as a marketing system for your business.

Three (3) Essential Ingredients Inside Your Marketing Funnel

There are three (3) essential ingredients that must go into your funnel for it to become a finely tuned marketing system and grow your business. Leaving any one of them out will cripple your marketing efforts and prevent your company from reaching its full potential and earning the profit you deserve to have from it.

Ingredient #1 – CONTENT

Without any marketing content in your funnel, you will not have a way to attract prospects into your story and marketing funnel or be able to keep the conversation going with your customers.

Your content keeps your story alive in the minds and hearts of your customers and continually invites them to go deeper into your funnel, which is something I will mention at least a few more times before we are done here.

To invite prospects into your marketing funnel and tell them your remarkable story, you need to develop and create compelling content that will move someone from prospect to customer as they move down your funnel.

Content creation must always be a strategic activity, which means you must always create your content with an objective in mind. Remember, your marketing funnel is a system and all your marketing content must have a specific purpose in moving someone deeper and deeper into your funnel and delivering a more meaningful experience for your customer each and every time.

Whimsical content creation is not a strategy and can do more harm than good. That is not to say that content created on a whim is not effective, just make sure as often as possible that it can be strategically placed within your marketing funnel to fulfill a specific purpose in the experience of your customers.

So let's get into some specific types of content that works for small businesses:

Video – Let's face it, video is engaging. It can be used in so many powerful ways to introduce people to your business, invite them into your marketing funnel, and move them deeper into it.

Every small business should have a video content strategy in place and should be making videos regularly. Not only is video engaging, entertaining, and educational, it is also loved by the search engines, which can get your business website ranked higher in search engines and thus allow prospects to find your business.

There are many different types of videos you could be creating for your business. Here is a list of some of them:

Introduction Video – A short video introducing your business and your unique story (value) proposition.

Product Demo – Short videos that teach people about your products and how to get the best use out of them.

Announcement – A video announcing your new product or service.

Success Stories – Also known as testimonial videos, but success stories sounds better because they are stories! Remember, facts tell; stories sell! Nothing will *sell* your business to others better than the success stories of your customers.

10x10x4 Videos – This concept was created by Mike Keonigs of Traffic Geyser. Here is how it is broken down – Ten (10) short videos are created answering the top ten (10) frequently asked questions your prospects and customers have. Ten (10) videos are created answering the top ten (10) questions they should be asking. Four (4) very short videos are created as calls to action that are attached at the ends of your frequently asked/should ask videos.

The 10x10x4 formula is a powerful video strategy that every small business should deploy. They will help with your search engine optimization as well as engage your audience and keep them moving down your funnel.

Creating videos is easy these days. Smart phones offer almost studio-quality video capabilities. The important thing is to be strategic in your video creation. Also make sure to plan your videos and also that they tell a story each time. Make sure the audio is top-quality. You can almost get away with poor quality video these days, but if your audio sucks, your video will most certainly suck too.

Books – A book is an amazing conversation starter. It is the ultimate business card. Imagine meeting a prospect that would be a perfect customer for your business and you happen to have your book with you. Most people are used to receiving a business card. Your prospect might even be thinking to themselves, "*Oh no! Is he going to hand me his business card?*"

Now imagine handing that prospect a copy of your book instead and even dog-earing a page that solves a specific problem the prospect mentioned. Can you imagine the rock star status you would have in the mind of that prospect? You would be an instant authority to that person. In a world of experts, the authority is the rock star!

A book is one of the most powerful forms of content there is. The old barriers to becoming a published author have been broken down. It is easy now to write a book or have it written for you and self-publish it to the Amazon Kindle platform and printed in paperback or hardcover. You no longer have to purchase hundreds or thousands of copies of your book. It is all printed on demand now. Your book is not printed until someone buys it and buying copies of your own book to hand out is only a couple of dollars.

Now you might be saying, *"But I'm not a writer!"*, or, *"I don't have anything to write about."* You can put that nonsense aside. You do not have to be a writer to have your own book and there is plenty for you to write about...or not write about.

What I mean is, you do not have to do the writing. Can you talk? If you can talk, you can create a book. Remember the 10x10x4 video creation strategy? You could have those videos transcribed and turned into a book.

The point is, it is super easy to create and publish your own book. You can do it all yourself or hire someone to help you do it. Make sure to hire someone that knows the book creation process and knows how to market you and your book effectively. Remember, you want to become an authority from your book. Make sure whomever you hire is able to do that for you.

Having your own book is a powerful way to get people into your marketing funnel.

Webinars – Webinars are one of the most powerful and effective marketing tools on the planet. It is basically a short seminar online. You can participate in and watch them on your computer, tablet, or smart phone.

Webinars can be used in a lot of ways. You can use them for educating your prospects and customers, selling products, or even both.

There are several webinar creation and hosting platforms out there and most of them are expensive. Google Hangouts are an incredible way to deliver great webinars and they are free to create. All you need is a Google account, a YouTube channel, and a webcam. You can run your webinar by being directly on camera or you can present a slideshow type webinar using Microsoft PowerPoint or Apple Keynote.

With Google Hangouts, your webinar is automatically recorded and uploaded to your YouTube channel. That gives you another video to use as part of your video creation strategy. You do not even have to have people attend your webinars live or at all. You can just use the Hangout platform for creating videos.

There are software tools out there that integrate with Google Hangouts to make them powerful and robust webinars with lots of customer engagement features.

You can find tools and other resources in my free resource guide by going to www.StoryEconomy.com.

Podcasts – Podcasts have been around for several years, but only recently have they proven to be an incredible way to create content for your business.

A podcast is like a radio show only it is recorded and uploaded to places like Apple's iTunes or to SoundCloud.com. People can then subscribe and listen to your podcast whenever you upload a new one. There are several successful podcast out there in all kinds of niches and their creators are making sizable incomes from them.

All you need to create a podcast is a decent recording device and a microphone. There are several different options for these like smart phones, tablets, or computers. It just depends on what works best for you.

For me, I do several interviews with successful entrepreneurs for my own podcast and I bought some professional recording equipment. I record the interviews over Skype and I use a recorder that works with Skype to record the interviews. I spent about $200 on a good USB microphone and other equipment that goes with it. You can spend more or less to create great podcasts.

Hosting a podcast gives you another way to create marketing content for your business. Your podcasts can also be re-purposed by being transcribed and turned into a book. Several successful entrepreneurs are already doing that and have created bestselling books from their podcasts.

Podcasts can be audio only or video as well. Just pick which one works best for your business and get started. One tip about podcasting is to make it a regular event. Your podcasts do not have to be any particular length of time. They can be quick 5-10 minute recordings and uploaded once per week, month, or whenever you want. Just make sure your audience knows that a new podcast will be available at a regular, specified day and time. Otherwise you could lose listeners and subscribers.

Blog – A blog is a great way for you to engage with your customers. You can easily craft a quick message on your blog and give your customers a little more information for them to consume. You can also use your blog to educate your customers about your products and services and answer questions your customers have.

Blogs are a perfect way to add fresh, relevant content into your marketing funnel. Again, if you do not want to write, have your podcast transcribed and use it for your blog content.

Your marketing content creation strategy will make or break your business. If you do not have a strategy in place, your competitors will. It is only a matter of time. More and more entrepreneurs are bringing their businesses into alignment with the current trends in marketing and storytelling and using current technology to deploy it. Is your business one of them?

A lack of good marketing will eventually kill your business. A properly set up marketing funnel with continual content flowing through it will make it thrive and grow like crazy.

The bottom line is this -You MUST have a content creation strategy in your business. You may be thinking that you do not have time to create content let alone develop a strategy for it. I am telling you right now that you cannot afford not to be creating fresh, relevant content on a regular basis. If you don't, your competitors will.

Start delegating the tasks in your business that you should not be doing in the first place. It is a lot cheaper to find someone to delegate to than it is to file bankruptcy. You do not necessarily have to always be the one who creates marketing content for your business, but you need to be the one that gets the ball rolling in the beginning.

Create a content strategy for your business and start creating the content to go in your funnel or hire a professional to do it.

Time is ticking...

Ingredient #2 – LOVE

Yes, I said it! Ingredient #2 is *love*, a very specific kind of love. You must absolutely love your customers. To love your customers, you must be attracting your perfect customers. Remember your perfect customer avatar? Well, that is who you want to fill your marketing funnel with because it is a lot easier to love your perfect customer as opposed to someone who is not. If you plan to be like Wal-Mart, then by all means, fill your funnel with everyone and try and satisfy all their crazy needs.

There is just no way around it. You will love those people who are perfect for your business. It will be easier to engage with them, sell to them, and tell your story to them.

If you do not love your customers, they will sense that and not have any love for you either. In the social media world, you cannot get away with not loving your customers. They will spread your lack of love all over their social media platforms and you will be left with a reputation nightmare.

When you love your customers, they love you back. They go deeper into your marketing funnel, they buy more products and buy more often, they share their experiences on their social networks, and send you more referrals.

If you do not love your customers, ask yourself why. Is it because your business is not attracting the perfect customer? Are you telling a forgettable story? What can you do to love your customers?

The Beatles said it best, "*Love is all you need!*" So love your customers, share great content with them, and watch your profits soar!

Ingredient #3 – PROSPECTS

You most definitely need prospects! Once you have plenty of initial content to fill your funnel and you have mixed in the right amount of love, you have to be actively filling your marketing funnel with perfect potential customers.

Finding People to fill Your Funnel

Having a continual source of new prospects is a crucial part of a thriving business. Too many businesses get into the trap of focusing on customers they already have and not balancing that with a steady flow of new prospects. That is where having a marketing funnel system in place makes all the difference.

In Chapter 6, I go into more detail about where to find prospects to fill your marketing funnel.

Prospects

Funnel image 3

Chapter 6

Designing Your Marketing Funnel

Now that you have the right ingredients in your marketing funnel, let's design a funnel so you get an idea of how the system could work in your business.

The first thing to consider is how you are going to persuade your prospects to enter the top of your funnel. This can be done by using some of the content you created that your customers consume inside your funnel or specifically created content that is solely used to invite people into your funnel. I recommend you create content specifically for inviting people into your funnel.

Free

When someone is attracted to your marketing funnel, you want to offer them something in exchange for their name and email address at the minimum. Any amount of contact info is great, but the minimum is their name and email.

The idea here is that you want to offer some kind of irresistible giveaway to your prospects for free for giving you their precious, guarded contact info. One of the most powerful words in sales and marketing is, *free*. Use that to your advantage while offering something of value to the prospect. Free does not mean cheap. Facebook marketing authority, Amy Porterfield says to pack your free giveaway with so much value that people would be willing to pay for it.

When I am fly fishing, I carry an assortment of artificial flies with me to use to attract trout in the streams I fish in. By carrying an assortment of flies, I know that I will have the appropriate fly for the stream conditions I am in. When I see a good spot on the stream where I know there are fish waiting, I cast my fly up stream and let it float by the waiting trout. Because I have selected an irresistible fly, the trout are so attracted to it and they go crazy while fighting to get it.

It is then up to me to give the fly a quick, gentle tug to set the hook in the fish's lip. Then I have to delicately, and with some finesse, guide the fish into my net.

The flies are like your free, irresistible giveaway. You want to select the appropriate offer for them and put it out there where they can see it and attract them to it. If you have selected the right offer, they will *bite*.

Every business should have an irresistible giveaway for the sole purpose of building an email list of their prospects and customers.

The next image of the funnel shows the prospect at the top of the funnel waiting to be attracted to your free offer.

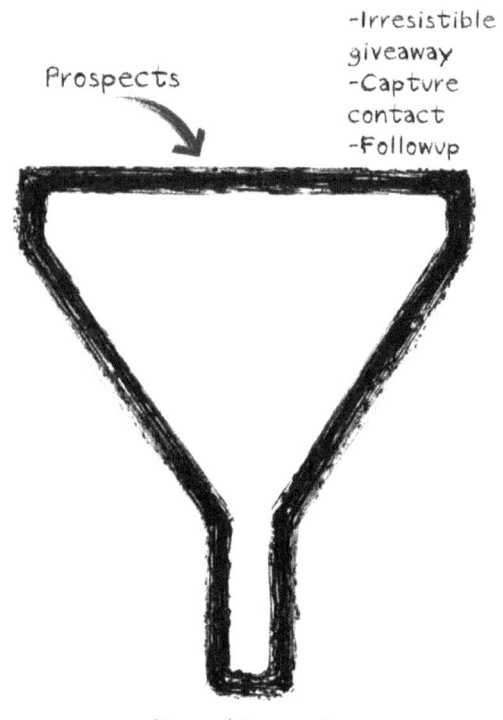

Funnel image 4

Now let's look at some of the types of free offers you can use to attract prospects into your marketing funnel:

Free report – One of the easiest things to create and offer to your prospects is a free report. Here are a couple of examples:

A roofing contractor could create a report titled, *3 Reasons Why Your Roof Keeps Leaking and How to Find the Right Roofing Contractor to Fix It...Permanently!* This is a perfect lead-in for a roofer to get a prospect interested in entering their funnel. A lot of people have roof leaks that have been fixed in the past, but the roof keeps leaking. It is a very frustrating experience that leaves homeowners feeling cheated and with little hope of any permanent solution.

The title of the report addresses a serious problem that the prospect is facing and a solution to fix the problem.

A car mechanic could create a report titled, *How to Avoid the One Mistake You are Making with Your Car That Could Cost You $1000s.* Lots of people neglect to get the oil in their vehicles changed at the appropriate mileage...usually every 3000-5000 miles depending on the year and make of their vehicle.

Neglecting to change the oil in your car can seriously decrease the life of the engine and cause all kinds of expensive problems. By educating prospects on what can happen to their cars if they do not get the oil changed, the prospect experiences a bit of fear that maybe it is better to get the oil changed on time instead of paying for an engine overhaul.

There are many creative ways to use free reports at the top of your funnel. Just remember that you want your prospects to take action and move deeper into your funnel so do not forget to include a call to action at the end of your free report or even a few times throughout the report. You need to tell them what to do next. If you assume they will just know what to do, your prospects will finish reading your report and move on to something else. I go deeper into why calls to action are crucial to your business later in Chapter 9.

Free eBook – An eBook is similar to a report except it is usually longer and written like a traditional book with a table of contents and chapters. A free eBook should be used to educate your prospects and help them with the problems they are experiencing by giving them the idea that there could be a solution. At the end of the eBook, show them how they can take the next step toward getting their problems solved with your products and services.

Blueprint – I am not talking about a blueprint for building a new house. I am talking about a blueprint that is a step-by-step guide to whatever. For a dentist, it could be a detailed guide for brushing your teeth to prevent cavities.

I know a chiropractor who created a blueprint that she uses to teach people how to properly sit at their desk while working to avoid certain back ailments. She also educates her customers about the necessity of getting up out of their chairs periodically throughout the day to keep their blood flowing.

A florist could create a blueprint that details how to make roses last five (5) days longer than normal or something like that.

Your blueprint does not have to look like a set of house plans. Make yours look like a set of plans for showing your prospects how to do something specific.

Videos – Here I am talking about videos again. Videos can be used in many different ways to get prospects to enter your marketing funnel and give their name and email address. You could turn your free report, ebook, and blueprint all into videos.

One way to use videos in your funnel is to create a video series. A video series is a series of videos that your prospects watch, either one after another or over the course of a few days. Your video series can even be spaced out over three to five emails.

Your videos can consist of information about your products or answers to frequently asked questions, or anything else you can come up with. You can get as creative or as simple as you would like with videos. Remember the 10x10x4 video formula I mentioned before? You could pull out three to five of those videos and put them into your video series.

Recently, I came across a great online training course for creating the best videos for your business. The course was created by *Do It Yourself Video Guy*, Caleb Wojcik. Actually, Caleb has three (3) course options from the full package to just an ebook. All three (3) options will give you great information on creating amazing video content for your business.

Another video guy I follow is, James Wedmore. Caleb is more of a video creation guy and James is too, but James has tons of great free and paid content on using videos to market your business and drive traffic to it.

James has a course called, *Video Traffic Academy*, as well as some others and they are all worth checking out. I have included info on these video courses in my resource guide at www.StoryEconomy.com

Audio – Many people like to listen to audio while driving, exercising, or just relaxing. One of the most powerful forms of audio is podcasts. Even though podcasting has been around for several years, many people still do not know what they are.

A podcast is basically like a radio show, except the podcast is recorded and then uploaded to an online podcast hosting company, which is similar to a website hosting company.

Then the podcast is added to iTunes, Sticher, or SoundCloud, or other podcast broadcasting platforms.

People can then go to iTunes or one of the other broadcasting platforms and subscribe to and download your podcast. I have my own podcast called, *Entrepreneur Jam*, which you can find under the same name at iTunes, Sticher.com, and SoundCloud.com. You can also listen at EJamPodcast.com

On *Entrepreneur Jam* I interview successful entrepreneurs, talk shop with experts, and talk about useful and effective marketing tools, techniques, and strategies for small businesses.

Producing your own podcast can lead to you becoming THE authority in your industry as well as a trusted advisor to those who follow you.

There are other forms of audio you can use, but podcasting is the most powerful and offers you the most return on investment, even if it is just your time.

Just like the other forms of content I described before for attracting people into your marketing funnel, you can use podcasts to attract them as well. One idea is to take your other content and turn it into a podcast. Do you have some videos? Strip out the audio and turn it into a podcast. Or, just leave the audio and video together and upload as a video podcast.

The same content in your special report can be read in a natural tone into a microphone, recorded, and created into an enticing podcast episode.

I will talk more about repurposing your content shortly, but right now, let's stay focused on more kinds of content for the top of your marketing funnel.

Webinars – Just like podcasts, webinars have been around for several years, but unlike podcasts, many people are familiar with webinars.

Webinars are a powerful tool for inviting people to go deeper into your funnel. Because webinars can be used in such broad and creative ways, they can be used at any point in your funnel, from the top down.

Webinars are like online seminars or interactive infomercials. They usually consist of one or more hosts and several attendees that show up to learn something and sometimes make purchases.

Webinars are also recorded, which adds to your video content. Not every small business will use webinars in their sales and marketing. A grocery store would not use webinars to talk about their eggs and milk or how a certain cereal will be on sale next week.

A local mechanic could host a webinar and show people how to perform simple car maintenance that he does not usually profit from. The mechanic could offer a special service at the end of the webinar or just keep the webinar educational only, with a call to action of course. Either way, it gives people value and keeps them engaged with that mechanic.

Webinars are a great way to help people get the most out of your products or services, especially if there is a learning curve. I use a service called LeadPages to create simple landing pages as part of my own marketing funnels. LeadPages continually hosts webinars to help it's customers get the most out of their software. I have included information about LeadPages in my resource guide at www.StoryEconomy.com. When you go to that URL, the page you see was created using LeadPages.

Email series – An email series is a versatile way to engage your prospects when they opt-in to your marketing funnel and want to hear more about your story.

An email series is a series of emails that are pre-written and put into an online autoresponder software. Using the autoresponder software you can then schedule out the emails so that the recipients receive them at specific intervals based on when they signed up for your email series at the top of your funnel. I go into more detail about autoresponders later in this chapter.

For example, an accountant could create an email series based on crucial tax tips for the coming tax season. She could create a five-part email series that delivers one tip per email and schedule the emails so that the prospect receives a new tip every day for five (5) days at a specified time of day.

The content and delivery timing of your email series will depend on your specific business and who your perfect customers are. It may be more appropriate for them to receive an email once per week or once per month. You can always take a survey from your existing customers and ask them what would be the appropriate amount of emails for your email series and what intervals are best. You can also ask them what kinds of information would have been most useful to them when they were first prospects at the top of your marketing funnel.

If an email series or email marketing in general seems a little over your head, you can always talk to an expert who is familiar with email marketing and creating marketing funnels.

Newsletter – I am hesitant to include newsletters as an irresistible giveaway. I am not sure they are all that irresistible anymore because everyone has a free newsletter and that is what they are using to attract people to enter their marketing funnels.

I receive about two (2) regular marketing-related newsletters by email about one or two times per month, but that is because I signed up for them several years ago when newsletters were still something people thought were irresistible. If I were signing up today, I am not sure I would be that excited to do it.

When everyone is offering the same thing, how do you know which one to choose? It is a lot like advertising in the Yellow Pages, when all the ads say the same thing, how do you know which plumber to choose?

I am not saying you cannot have a newsletter, but maybe make it something you offer to people after they are already in your funnel. Once people know, like, and trust you, then a newsletter can be a great way to keep in touch with them.

Consultation – Depending on what your profession is, offering a free consultation can be an incredible way to attract prospects into your funnel. But...

There's always a big but. I heard that in a movie one time. It is true as far as free consultations are concerned. So here is the but...

You can offer a free consultation, but...give that prospect the most amazing consultation ever! Remember, you are telling a story to your prospects and in your free consultation, they are deciding if they want to experience more of your story or run away screaming.

Here is a perfect piece of advice: In your free consultations, give away so much value that your prospect will open their wallet and pay you.

You can be creative with your consultations. You can do them in person, over the phone, or even over Skype.

117

Physical Product – I do not want you to think that you cannot offer a physical product to attract people to your marketing funnel.

One guy I know who does very well marketing online and consulting small businesses, offers two (2) different free, printed books online that he ships to people. They are short books (about 80 pages), but they each offer so much actionable advice that I will bet most people would pay a lot of money for it.

You can offer any kind of physical product you want to attract people into your funnel. It is just a matter of what works for your business and prospects.

You now have some ideas of the kinds of giveaways you can offer your prospects to attract them into your marketing funnel. I will bet you could sit down and think of several more that work for your prospects. What is fun about it is you can get super creative and come up with all kinds of different giveaways. I would suggest coming up with several ideas and then testing them against each other to find out which ones work the best. Continue to do that over time. You may have a giveaway that works for a while, which is great, but continue to test those offerings against others to make sure you are always offering the best one.

Repurposing Your Content

Earlier I mentioned the possibility of repurposing your marketing content into other formats. The reason for repurposing your content is because people have preferences in the ways they digest content. For some people, text based content works for them, while others may prefer video. A lot of people these days are listening to podcasts while they commute. That is sure a lot easier than reading content while driving and certainly a lot safer.

The easiest way to think of repurposing your marketing content is to take the content you have and turn it into the other forms of content. For example, turn your podcast into a video and written form like a short ebook or report. Turn your video into a podcast and written form. And turn your written content into both video and audio.

Again, by repurposing your content, you will appeal to more people and give them the opportunity to consume your content in ways that work for them.

The Two (2) Most Important Components in Your Marketing Funnel

In order for prospects and customers to receive your irresistible giveaway and any other marketing content along their journey down your marketing funnel, you have to have two (2) key components in place to make that happen.

Opt-in form – This is a form you must have on the home page of your website or lead-capture page where people can leave their name and email address in exchange for your irresistible giveaway. This is the entry point to your marketing funnel. Without this in place, you are basically placing a cap on the top of your funnel and locking it down. You will learn more about this in Chapter 9 about funnel interrupts.

When you place an opt-in form on your website, it needs to be placed above the fold. The fold is the bottom most part of the web browser that you can see without scrolling down. When a prospect comes to your web page, they need to see your-opt-in form right there in front of them without having to scroll down the page to see it. So right there in front of their eye balls is your irresistible giveaway and a way for them to get it.

Another good place for your opt-in form is at the bottom of the web page. That way if for some reason your prospect does scroll down the page they will see your opt-in form a second time and may leave their contact info at that point.

Later on in the funnel interrupts chapter, I talk about how your website must be either a responsive or mobile optimized website. Basically this means that when someone views your website on a mobile device like a smartphone, your website will fit their screen without them having to pinch and zoom to read your site content.

Recently I heard a statistic that if a website is not optimized for the mobile experience that 47% of people will not return to that website in the future. Can your business afford a 47% drop off like that?

Now imagine that your website is mobile ready and your visitors see your irresistible giveaway on their phone with an easy way to get it. Not only will you avoid that huge drop off in traffic, but you will be building a list of prospects as well.

Autoresponder – The opt-in form on your website has to have some kind of functionality to it, right? What happens after prospects opt-in for your free giveaway? Good question!

After a prospect opts-in for your irresistible giveaway your autoresponder takes over. An autoresponder is a software program that responds automatically to actions like someone opting-in on your website. There are many different kinds of autoresponder software services and they all do pretty much the same thing with some having more bells and whistles than others.

Here is how it works: An autoresponder is an automated email solution that allows you to create pre-written emails that are sent when a specific action is taken, like a prospect opting-in for your giveaway. If you have ever sent someone an email and you received a reply back that says that person is on vacation or out of the office, that is an autoresponder message at work. The person you have sent the email to created an email message that is sent right back to you to let you know they are not available to reply in that moment.

Autoresponders are very versatile in that you can use them to send one email or as many as you want. Let's say your prospect opts-in for your giveaway and you want to keep your business fresh in their minds so that they will go deeper into your marketing funnel. You can pre-write a series of emails that will automatically be sent to the prospect over a period of time that you pre-select, like one email per week for five (5) weeks.

Once your prospects opt-in on your website, they will then receive and email from you once a week for the next five (5) weeks automatically. And this is what will happen with every prospect that opts-in. They will receive the same email sequence that your other prospects do. What is cool about autoresponders is that you can set them up to include the prospect's first name at the top of the email or anywhere else you want to address them by name. It gives your emails a personal touch. People are more aware now that they are receiving a pre-written email, but they still like seeing their name at the top.

Another function of an autoresponder software service is that whenever someone opts-in for your giveaway, they are automatically entered into your email database on a list that you pre-designate.

When you build an email list of your prospects and customers, you can offer them more great content as well as options to buy from you.

When you have an opt-in form and an autoresponder system in place, you have a powerful way of keeping in touch with your prospects and inviting them to go deeper into your marketing funnel.

Some businesses rely heavily on networking-type events to fill their funnels, so how would that work with an opt-in form. There are a couple of ideas of how to accomplish this.

Ask prospects you meet at networking events to opt-into your email list right on your cell phone. Before you attend, bring up your website with your opt-in form on the screen and when you meet someone you would like to keep in touch with, mention your free giveaway and ask if they would enter their info on your phone.

You can also just ask permission to add prospects to your mailing list. That is just good networking manners anyway, but also a way for you to add prospects to your funnel and mailing list.

Some autoresponders will not allow you to manually enter a new prospect into your email list, but others will. I have included a list of the most popular autoresponders in my resource guide at www.StoryEconomy.com.

A Quick Rant About Irresistible Giveaways

You have to get creative when thinking of your irresistible giveaway to offer prospects when they first come to your marketing funnel. Doing what everyone else is doing will make your business a commodity, which means you will always compete on price. When you find a unique and compelling giveaway, that becomes irresistible and you are operating as a proprietary business, which is a business that, *thinks different*, and has a remarkable story to tell.

I have mentioned the Yellow Pages a few times in this book. Just the other day, I received one of those envelopes in the mail stuffed with slips of paper ads from local businesses and franchises. I get those a few times per month along with the local ad magazines. Most of the businesses are advertising in each of the mailers and the ad magazines hoping to get the exposure they need so people will call them. It seems like panicky desperation to me.

Very few of the businesses that advertise in those spaces have a marketing funnel in place. The ones that do, have interrupts in their funnels rendering them useless.

The other thing is there are several businesses of the same industry with ads in each mailer and magazine. Carpet cleaning companies are the dominant one, all with the same ad. You could easily use the platitude test I talked about earlier in the book to prove that the ads are ineffective. I could swap out the names of each company and place them on their competitor's ad and you would not know that I had done so.

Businesses that advertise in the Yellow Pages, mailers, and ad magazines are all focused on getting more customers to get sales instead of the reverse, making sales to get customers. It is all evident in the lack of marketing funnels.

Even websites like Groupon and Living Social are basically offering the same thing to all these local businesses that place ads with them, a new way to get people to buy, but without the intent to build a lasting relationship with those buyers. And the people that do not buy, a lot of them go to the company's website for more information. What do they see there? I will tell you what they do not see, any kind of irresistible giveaway. Again, no marketing funnel is in place.

Why would you want to advertise like all your competitors in places where they are all advertising too? Tell a better story than that. Make your story remarkable by making it different.

Be the *purple cow*!

Chapter 7

Where to Find Prospects to Fill Your Funnel

In order to fill your marketing funnel with prospects, you have to know where they are so you can attract them to your story and into the top of your funnel.

Fly-fishing has always been more enjoyable for me when I am fishing in a river I know has lots and lots of fish. After all, it's called fishing, not casting. My fishing philosophy is, 'Go where the fish are.'

Think of finding your prospects like fly-fishing. Go where your prospects are. This comes back to positioning your business and story where your prospects are. Being anywhere else is like practicing attracting prospects. It sounds silly because it is silly.

It is impossible for me to go into every single possibility of where your prospects might be without knowing your specific industry. For the sake of time and a 5000 page book, I will just go into a few options of where your prospects might be waiting for you.

Social Media

Covering every social media platform for marketing purposes would require a series of books and there are plenty of authorities out there who have written awesome books on marketing through social media. I will mention them as we go along.

Facebook – There is a very real possibility that your prospects are on Facebook because almost everyone in the world is on Facebook. Facebook has been a great way for businesses to position their stories and be found by their perfect prospects.

Just like Google, Facebook changes all the time in regards to how easy and cheap it is for a business to reach prospects and customers. Because Facebook is a publicly traded company, they have shareholders that they have to please, which means that Facebook has to make money, lots of money.

Because Facebook has to make lots of money, they are transitioning away from free organic traffic, to making it almost impossible for businesses to reach their prospects and customers without paying for ads. That is not necessarily a bad thing, especially for small businesses.

A lot of businesses will either reduce their focus on Facebook as a marketing platform or ditch it altogether. Some will get creative with Facebook ads and continue to thrive as their story gets more exposure and engagement.

It is worth creating a Facebook marketing strategy for your business based on the amount of people actively using the platform, especially if your perfect customers are on there.

There are several training courses online that teach Facebook marketing. I have been following Amy Porterfield for a while and I listen to her podcast often. She is a well-known and recognized Facebook marketing authority. You can find more info about Amy in my resource guide at www.StoryEconomy.com.

Twitter – Twitter to me, seems like Facebook's cousin; they don't look alike, but they act in similar ways.

As Facebook transitions away from free organic traffic and into more of a paid traffic model, Twitter can still work for organic traffic to a point as well as paid traffic. Paid traffic on Twitter is still less expensive than Facebook, but that could change the day after I publish this book.

Because everything online is changing regularly, you have to stay up to date on what is new and what is working or not working. Testing different platforms and ads will help you in keeping your advertising costs down on the various social media platforms.

Another great resource on social media marketing is Gary Veynerchuk's book, *Jab, Jab, Jab, Right Hook – How to Tell Your Story in a Noisy Social World*. Of course I loved the book. It's about storytelling.

Gary V (as he is also known) gives many examples of how to tell your story and market your business on the top social media platforms. He does not have any online courses that I know of, but reading his books and watching his videos will give you plenty of information to go on. Gary loves Twitter and uses it masterfully. Just search for him online and you will find tons of info to keep you busy for a while.

Pinterest and Instagram – I won't go into details about these two fairly new and powerful social media platforms, but I know a guy named, Jason Miles, who wrote two amazing books on these two platforms called, *Pinterest Power* and *Instagram Power*, and you can find both on Amazon.com.

There is also an online training course called, *The Power of Pinning*, created by Pinterest marketing authority, Melanie Duncan. I recommend you dive into the books and course suggestions I have offered here. If Pinterest and Instagram will work for marketing your story, then it is worth looking into the best info.

You can find info about The Power of Pinning course in my free resource guide at www.StoryEconomy.com.

Social media marketing can drive lots of traffic to your marketing funnel. Here are a couple more ways to drive traffic to your funnel and keep it filled with prospects.

Referrals – There may be no greater way to fill your marketing funnel than with referrals from happy customers. Every other form of traffic requires you to attract people into your funnel. With referrals, you have a happy storyteller bringing their family and friends to you, which means they have pre-qualified you and your business.

Does it get any better than that? Many times, a referral prospect will enter your funnel and go straight to a purchase point. Even though they may bypass your initial point of entry into your funnel, you will still collect their contact info, but they end up deeper in your funnel right from the start. In case you were wondering, that's a good thing!

Getting to the point where your business receives a steady amount of referrals takes time in building relationships with your prospects while turning them into customers.

Networking – Networking can be a fantastic way to fill your funnel. For certain professions like real estate agents, attorneys, accountants, and financial planners, networking can be the life-blood of their businesses. Many kinds of businesses can benefit from networking. It just takes a time commitment and a commitment to growing your business.

You can do a search in your local area for networking events. You can find events that are casual and groups that are more structured that require a commitment. The best thing is to go to some of the events in your area and find which ones work best for you and your business.

Go to networking events to give, not to receive. Networking is a relationship building activity. Those who get that are usually successful.

Four (4) Tips About Networking

1. Business cards – Make sure to bring plenty of business cards when you go to networking events. Most people are still accustomed to exchanging cards and until you have a book to hand out, keep plenty of cards with you.

2. Wait until they ask – Never give your business card to anyone until they ask you for it. People are not interested in you until you are interested in them. Genuinely get to know people you meet at networking events and give them incredible value. When people ask you for your business card, they are interested in what you have to offer.

3. Now it's your turn to ask them – Remember, networking events are a great way to fill your marketing funnel by adding prospects to your mailing lists, both email and traditional mail. The important thing is to ask permission of the prospects you meet if you can add them to your mailing list.

Adding someone to your mailing list without their permission is like handing them your business card without them asking for it. It's just bad form.

4. Follow up – You are going to be drilled on this point later in Chapter 10, but it is essential to mention it here in regards to networking. You can attend every networking event in town, but it will not do you or your business any good if you do not follow up with the people you meet. If you neglect to follow up, you will just end up with a desk over-run by hundreds of business cards.

Do not think that you can just throw them in a box and follow up six (6) months later. Sometimes when my dog has left evidence of being naughty, I want to scold her. The problem is, she has no idea what she is being scolded for. People you meet at networking events are the same way. Although you are not going to scold them, if you do not follow up with them for several months, they will forget about you and give you a funny look, like my dog.

My favorite way to follow up with people I meet at networking events is with greeting cards. I like to use SendOutCards to send greeting cards. I am not talking about those lame ecards that get sent through email. I am talking about actual physical cards with a stamp that gets delivered by the postal service.

SendOutCards is an online greeting card service that allows you to create and send greeting cards from your computer. You can choose from thousands of pre-made cards or design your own with your own photos and images.

I have several cards that I had professionally designed that I use for different situations when I meet people, like networking. I just choose the card I want to send, add a personal message, click a couple buttons, and it is sent in the mail the next day.

People still like to get mail and greeting cards are their favorite. You can find out more about using SendOutCards in the resource list that is included in the book bonuses at www.StoryEconomy.com.

One hot tip about using greeting cards to follow up is to include a soft call to action in the card. Invite the recipient to get more information on your website or invite them to a landing page to get a free video series or some other high-value content. Remember, it is about getting prospects into your funnel.

You have to make following up part of your funnel filling strategy. When you meet people at networking events, you have not actually gotten them into your marketing funnel. You get them in by following up.

Search – People are looking for your business online. Can they find you? Ranking high in search engines like Google can give your business exposure and a good source of prospects into your marketing funnel.

There are different ways to get found through search. There are organic search results, which are the search results you find in the middle of the page on a Google search. There are paid search results, which show up in the form of ads above the organic results and on the right side of those results as well.

Usually most people look through the organic search results before focusing on paid ads. Finding a marketing consultant that can assist you with rich, content-based search engine optimization (SEO) could get your business found in front of your prospects when they search for you online.

Advertising – This is not a book about advertising, but I will give you a few examples of how you can fill your marketing funnel using different kinds of ads.

Like I mentioned about search, there are paid search results that show up in the form of tiny ads. Those are pay-per-click ads, or PPC. Sometimes this can be a good source of new prospects into your funnel. Again, consult with an authority on PPC type advertising.

As I mentioned earlier, Facebook and Twitter are incredible sources for filling your funnel. Facebook and Twitter ads can be targeted to your exact customer avatar. On Google, you have to wait for someone to type in the keywords related to your business in the search bar and then hope your business shows up in front of them. On Facebook, you can set up an ad campaign to show up right in front of your target audience. There is a lot of potential for setting up some powerful marketing funnels through Facebook.

Consult with someone knowledgeable on setting up marketing funnels on Facebook.

Print ads can still be a viable source of prospects for your business if they are set up correctly as part of your marketing funnel. It all depends on where the ad is being placed. Yellow Pages and print ads like that may not be the best option. Remember, you are advertising right next to your competitors in the Yellow Pages. Print ads should be well thought out and have very distinct calls to action that drive prospects into your funnel.

Trade shows – A trade show can be an exciting event that sends a lot of prospects into your marketing funnel. The secret to a successful event is how well you follow up with all those people in your funnel. Without a system for following up during and after the trade show, your whole investment in the event can be a waste. Using trade shows to fill your marketing funnel is a lot like networking events. Without follow up, it is a waste of time and money.

The people at Instant Customer have an amazing system for following up at events like trade shows. Their system completely automates the whole process of gathering prospects into your funnel and following up with them throughout the event as well as after. Check out Instant Customer in the book bonuses at www.StoryEconomy.com.

Joint Ventures – An often-overlooked source of new prospects is through joint venture deals with other businesses. For example, a company that sells BBQ sauce could benefit from a joint venture deal with a company that sells barbecues.

The barbeque company could do a promotion to their list of customers about the best BBQ sauce in town and receive a percentage of the sales of the sauce to it's customers.

The barbeque company benefits by offering something that complements their barbeques and makes the customers' experience so much better.

The BBQ sauce company benefits by adding a bunch of new prospects into its funnel. It is a win/win deal and these types of deals are easy to set up. If it sounds intimidating to you, find someone who gets it to broker the deal for you.

Books – A book is a powerful way to establish yourself as an authority in your industry. It can also be a great way to ad prospects into your funnel. As I said before, a book is a fantastic conversation starter.

Depending on what kind of book you have, you can invite people into your marketing funnel right inside your book by placing calls to action inside the content. For example, if you are an interior designer and you have a book about choosing the best furniture for your space, you could have links or your website address inside your book. You could invite people to go to your website for more information and capture their contact info, thus adding them into your marketing funnel.

Another benefit of a book is that it can lead to speaking engagements, which are another source of new prospects into your marketing funnel.

Video – Video is a powerful form of content that can drive serious amounts of prospects into your funnel. Again, this is not a book about specific types of funnel filling sources, but neglecting to mention video as a traffic source would just be mean.

Videos that are done right, with a quality picture and audio, and a specific call to action can be a continual source of new prospects for your business. They also have a powerful effect on search engine optimization. Google owns YouTube, which is the number one video site on the web. This means that Google loves video and well-made videos with engaging content even more. And when Google loves videos, they rank them high in their search results.

Video is not an option anymore. Make videos or your business will die a slow death. The YouTube authority I mentioned before, James Wedmore, has lots of content about finding prospects through video marketing. Again, I have included his info in the books bonuses at www.StoryEconomy.com.

Direct Mail – Even good old-fashioned direct mail still has its place in marketing. It is especially effective when keeping the conversation alive with your customers. When the internet and email went mainstream back in the mid-1990s, the use of direct mail started to taper off. After all, it was a lot easier and more affordable to send email and get people to your website.

Direct mail is still a powerful way to keep in touch and continue marketing to your customers and even to get new ones.

Dan Kennedy, who is one of the top marketing leaders in the world, wrote a book called, *NO B.S: Grassroots Marketing – The Ultimate No Holds Barred, Take No Prisoners Guide to Growing Sales and Profits of Local Small Businesses.* In Chapter 9 of the book, Dan lists the following headlines about the use of direct mail:

The Postman as Your Salesman – Using the Most Reliable Small-business Marketing Media – Direct Mail

Marry Direct Mail With all Other Grassroots Marketing

Use Direct Mail to Nurture and Maintain Relationships with Customers

Try and tell Dan Kennedy direct mail is dead and he will likely spit in your face...or worse. If you make it out alive, try and tell it to Google too. Google sends millions of direct mail pieces a year to businesses promoting its business tools, like Google Adwords advertising.

If it's good enough for Dan and Google, it's good enough for your business too.

Perhaps the most important headline I mentioned from Dan's book is the part about maintaining relationships with customers. That's the whole idea and reason behind the continual engagement you have with your customers...maintaining the relationship. And not just maintaining it, but nurturing it. You cannot maintain the relationship without continually engaging your customers and keeping the conversation alive.

Direct mail is a key part of it.

There are numerous ways to use direct mail in your continual marketing message, but this book could not fit it all in. I would suggest following Dan Kennedy and read what he has to say about it.

One of the headlines I mentioned earlier from his book, *Marry Direct Mail With all Other Grassroots Marketing*, is discussed further when Dan says:

"Every grassroots strategy, tactic, and method...can be aided before, during, or after it's use by direct mail."

So again, the emphasis is on direct mail as one of your most powerful forms of marketing media cannot be overlooked, as well as its use in your follow-up marketing.

Chapter 8

How to Invite Prospects to go Deeper into Your Marketing Funnel and Turn them into Customers

Now that you are attracting lots of prospects into your marketing funnel, it is time to invite them to go deeper and enjoy a more meaningful experience of your story.

Here are some examples of business owners who created marketing funnel systems in their businesses:

Rare Coin Dealer/Investor

A perfect example of someone inviting customers to go deeper into their marketing funnel is a story I remember that was shared by Jay Abraham about a client of his who is a rare coin dealer and investor.

Jay brokered a joint venture deal between a financial services company and client of his that is a rare coin dealer/investor.   Through the deal, the rare coin dealer was able to send out a newsletter to the clients of the financial services company and gained access to thousands of potential customers. In the newsletter he sent out a deal for a starter investment coin collection for less than $100. Several hundred people bought the starter collection and the dealer made a nice profit. That was a first tier purchase. That is the first point down the funnel after a prospect is attracted to and enters the funnel and then makes their first purchase.

Some time later, the coin dealer sent out another offer to his list of customers who bought the starter coin collection and offered them a bigger set of coins with greater value and a higher purchase price around $500. Less people bought the second offer, but there were still hundreds of customers who bought the second offer.

The coin dealer continued to invite his customers to go deeper into his marketing funnel. As they became more experienced coin collectors and investors, he offered them more opportunities to go deeper into his marketing funnel with bigger coin sets and higher price points. At one point I believe the dealer sold a coin investment opportunity at around $50,000. Of course, not all of his customers bought that deal, but the ones who did purchase, were entrenched deep into the dealer's funnel and story.

Everyone wins in a situation like that. The customers of the dealer win because they grow their investment portfolio in rare coins. The dealer wins by gathering new prospects into his funnel and grows a new customer base of happy investors.

Rare Coin Dealer's Marketing Funnel

Free newsletter

Invitation to purchase starter coin investment kit for $100

Invited to buy next level coin investment for $2500

Invited to buy next level coin investment for $500

Invited to buy next level coin investment for $50,000

Funnel image 5

Diabetic Smart Phone App

As a type 1 diabetic, I have the super fun opportunity of checking my blood sugar all day, monitoring what I eat and how often I exercise, and taking regular insulin injections. It is a fulltime job managing diabetes if you want to live long and to do so takes a lot of work.

One thing I have to do is track my blood sugar levels and how much insulin I am taking daily. Luckily, we have technology so I do not have to carry around a notebook to log all my info, which I would probably lose anyway.

Recently, I downloaded and app on my iPhone called, *mySugr*. With this app I can input each blood sugar reading throughout the day as well as any insulin injections I require. I can make notes about what I have eaten and what I did for exercise. It also gives me a seven (7) day average blood sugar reading which keeps me on track. When it is time to go to the doctor, I can print off all of my data from the app and take it with me.

The app is also fun and engaging with a gamification side to it. Gamification is a new way of saying that there is a game element to something and that it's fun.

Most of the time when I download an app I do not have to create an account with my name and email. With mySugr, I created an account. What happened next was awesome!

The app I downloaded from mySugr was a free version of the app. After I downloaded the app, I received an email welcoming me to the diabetic clan. Everyone at mySugr is diabetic too. It's pretty cool when you are living similar stories like that.

A week after I downloaded the free app, I received an email asking how my experience with the mySugr app was going and if I wanted to upgrade to the pro version of the app. It was a pretty soft sell, which I assume was strategic because I was still new in their marketing funnel. It is likely I will get another email soon with more of a push for me to upgrade to the pro version. I am going to upgrade anyway, but I am curious to see what they will do to invite me to go deeper into their funnel. After all, I am a little obsessed with marketing funnels.

Jim Cockrum

Jim is a friend and mentor of mine who owns the title of the most trusted online entrepreneur as noted by internet marketing watchdog, *IM Report Card*. He is a bestselling author, coach, and mentor to tens of thousands of people around the world. Jim is the world's most sought after authority on the power of email marketing and growing an email list of raving fans.

Now I am sure Jim will hate that I am building him up so much here, but he deserves the praise. I first learned about marketing funnels from a video Jim created back in 1997. Jim has been selling and marketing online for over ten (10) years and has perfected the marketing funnel and telling an amazing story within it.

I first entered Jim's marketing funnel back in 2008. Actually, it was my Dad that entered the funnel first. He signed up for Jim's online newsletter and showed it to me one day. My Dad was so excited about this newsletter he received in his email that had an audio recording in it. My Dad clicked the play button and Jim started speaking and sharing useful tips about online marketing, like he always does with his audience.

My Dad forwarded Jim's email to me and I signed up for Jim's newsletter. About twice per month after that, I received Jim's newsletter that was short, but packed with the most powerful, free tips on topics from email marketing to selling products on Amazon. About every fourth or fifth contact from Jim, he would offer a product like an ebook or training course for creating success as an entrepreneur.

Jim has always been masterful at inviting people to go deeper into his marketing funnel, and always with the highest integrity and only when people were ready. It's a little funny, but I did not actually buy anything from Jim until he put an auction on eBay for a chance to be personally coached by him. He had put up a similar auction two (2) years previously that had been won by one of his students for the whopping price of $35,000. I remember wishing I had the money to bid on that auction.

Sure enough, a couple years later, Jim put up another auction for his coaching services and I won, although I did not pay anything close to $35,000, I still paid several thousand dollars. That was money well spent. Because Jim created such an efficient marketing funnel, I made a purchase when I was ready. I have met the most amazing people since then, including Jim, and have grown as an entrepreneur in so many ways as a benefit of Jim's coaching.

Because Jim Cockrum created and perfected his marketing funnel, tens of thousands of people's lives have been changed. People that were once struggling in jobs they hated now have freedom as full time entrepreneurs. Single moms are supporting their families using Jim's teachings. Over worked dads are now coming home to be with their families, watch their kids grow up, and earn a full time income as successful business owners.

It's A Conversation

Remember this, when you are inviting prospects to go deeper into your marketing funnel, you are basically asking them permission to carry on a conversation with you. That is what marketing is. It is a continual conversation with prospects and customers about your story.

As you continue the conversation with your customers always ask yourself this question I learned from marketing whiz, Joe Polish, "*What's the most natural next step for someone to take to go deeper into your marketing funnel?*"

Keeping the conversation going with your customers is what your marketing is all about.

As my friend, Bryan Elliott, of BehindTheBrand.tv, says, "*Marketing is storytelling.*"

Chapter 9

Funnel Interrupt

This is the part where I warn you against creating an incomplete funnel or what I call *funnel interrupts*.

You know when you call a company that uses an automated phone system and it navigates you through to the person you want to talk to?   Yeah, I don't either...because when do you ever call a company and get through to who you *really* want to speak with?

"Press 1 for customer service, press 2 for tech support, press 3 to be taken to a new menu of options that will cause you to bleed from your eyes."

Somehow we lost touch as a society and automated our phone systems that interrupt our lives and what should be a natural thing to do...*just talk to a real person.*

This kind of interrupt happens in the marketing funnels of most small businesses.   Sure, they attract you to their funnels and then send you away with nothing but a scrunched up, confused look on your face.

That is just unacceptable and totally unnecessary.   When prospects are attracted to your marketing funnel, it should be easy for them to enter it and naturally progress deeper into it.

The inability for prospects to enter and move deeper into your marketing funnel is called a funnel interrupt.   Here are some examples of funnel interrupts that are affecting the growth of small businesses everywhere:

No 'opt-in' form on your website – This is a simple form on the home page of your site where people can leave their name and email in exchange for something from your business. Another interrupt like this would be an opt-in form that is too small, does not offer anything in exchange for contact info, or in below the fold, which is the bottom portion of your website that is out of view when someone lands on your site.

Non-responsive or mobile optimized website – Responsive web design is all the rage these days and rightly so. A responsive website is a site that responds to the device it is being viewed on and adjusts accordingly. If someone is viewing a responsive site on their smart phone, then the site fits to their phone screen and everything is easy to read and view.

A non-responsive website can interrupt your funnel like nothing else. It causes people to have to take extra steps in order to view your content by turning their phones sideways or adjusting the size of your site on their phone screen. These days, people have shorter and shorter attention spans and the thought of having to take extra, unnecessary steps to view your site is plain ridiculous to them.

One thing that drives me nuts is clicking on a link to a website within the Facebook app on my iPhone and ending up on a non-responsive or non-mobilized site. I cannot turn my phone to make the site bigger in the Facebook app. To do so, I have to open the website in a browser and that is another unnecessary step I do not want to take and neither do most other people.

Make your website responsive or you will experience funnel interrupt and your customers will choose out of your funnel.

Non-responsive email text – When I read emails on my phone, there is nothing more annoying than text that is too small to read. With today's technology and email software, there is no excuse for emails with tiny text. Again, it causes people to take unwanted extra steps in order to view your content. Don't do that to them. Make it easy and make sure your emails show up in an easily readable form.

No social media follow-up – I see this far too often, especially with authority-types with loyal followings. They will post something engaging to their fan page and get a conversation started with their fans and customers. Then it's as if they leave the conversation all together. The authority never comes back in to engage in the conversation they started.

If you start a conversation on your social media platforms, do not leave your customers to talk to themselves. Keep the conversation going by jumping back into it. You do not have to respond to or like every single comment, but let your customers know you are still there. They will love you for it.

Lack of marketing content – This leads to long lapses in engagement and follow up. If you do not create regular, high-value content, you will not have anything to share with your customers and they will not move further down your marketing funnel. Remember this...*people follow those who follow up.*

You follow up with your customers by having great content to share with them.

No calls to action – In all of your content you must include at least one call to action that tells your prospects and customers what to do next. If you neglect to include a call to action in every piece of your marketing content, people will not go deeper in your funnel. Believe it or not, people need to be told what to do next. If you have an amazing product for sale but you neglect to tell people where and how they can buy it, you will be out of business before you know it. Always make it easy for people to take the natural next step down your marketing funnel. If you offer a free report, at the end of the report, tell the reader what to do next. In all of your videos, give the viewer a call to action that leads them further down your marketing funnel.

Not asking for the sale – I know, it's hard to believe people in business would forget to ask for the sale. I do not believe anyone really forgets to ask for the sale. I believe they are just afraid. Asking for the sale is the most important call to action in your business.
There is a term floating around these days that I first heard from Seth Godin called, *impostor syndrome*. It is basically the fear someone has that they are an impostor and that there is no way anyone would ever want to hear about anything they have to say or buy anything they have to sell. I call it the *George McFly syndrome*.

George McFly was a main character in the movie, *Back to the Future*, who said, "What if they say no? What if they say I'm no good? I just don't think I can take that kind of rejection." If you are not asking for the sale, look in the mirror and see if George McFly is staring back at you.

Anything that prevents your customer from naturally taking the next step through your marketing funnel is a funnel interrupt and must be dealt with right away. Having all the pieces in place within your marketing funnel will prevent funnel interrupts from happening. Analyze your funnel and see if it has any of the interrupts I mentioned here.

There is one more funnel interrupt I want to mention, it is the worst one of all, and it deserves special attention. Therefore, it has been included in the next chapter.

Moving on...

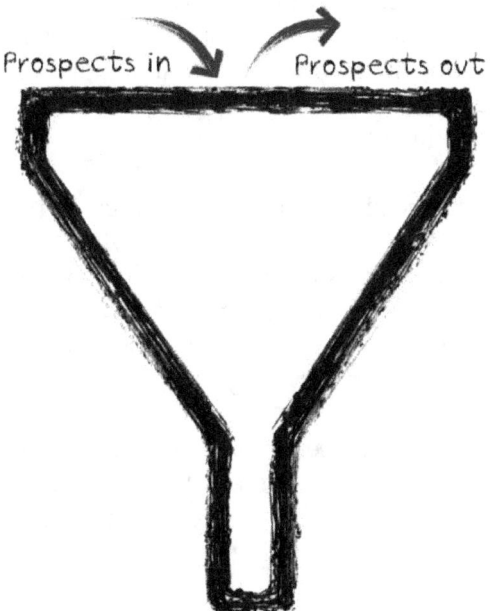

Funnel image 6

Chapter 10

The #1 Action that Keeps Your Funnel Flowing...or Completely Destroys It!

If you have ever gone fishing before, it is highly likely that you used a fishing net to scoop up your fish after you caught it. Can you imagine what would happen if you cut a hole in the bottom of your net? Fish would swim in and fish would swim out.

This is the sad reality of so many businesses today. They are essentially fishing for customers with holes in their nets. Think about it. All the time, effort, and money that is spent on acquiring new customers and there is a hole in their net. There is no system in place for keeping the customers around for very long.

If it does not make sense to have a hole in your fishing net, then it does not make sense to have holes in your marketing either. The holes in your marketing are funnel interrupts and there is nothing that interrupts a marketing funnel more than this:

Neglecting to follow up with your prospects and customers!

Let me explain it this way...

The Structure of Your Story

Every great story has a basic structure to it, the beginning, the middle, and the end. I know, you were expecting something more elaborate than that, but the structure of a story is that simple. Every great story ever told followed that same structure and it's the same structure you are following in the telling of your story inside your marketing funnel.

Now I want you to imagine this. Imagine if George Lucas structured the story of Star Wars so that shortly after we are introduced to Luke Skywalker as the hero of the story, Luke died by driving his land speeder off a cliff. That would have been a stupid story and we would have asked for our money back.

That sad scenario is the same story that too many businesses are telling every day. They attract prospects into their marketing funnel, turn them into customers and then interrupt the funnel by ignoring them.

Before, During, and After

Several years ago, I was watching a video of Jay Abraham and in that video he talked about the concept of finding what a customer needs before, during, and after they buy from a business.

I thought it was the most brilliant piece of business and marketing advice I had ever heard up to that point. It opened my mind to the idea of the business/customer relationship and that it should be an enduring connection.

It's the Dan Kennedy mindset again..."*You don't get a customer to make a sale; you make a sale to get a customer.*"

Recently though, I had a huge breakthrough with this before, during, and after mindset. I realized that it is not about what the customer needs before, during, and after the sale, although that is part of it. I was reading a report I downloaded off of ILoveMarketing.com, created by Dean Jackson and Joe Polish. They presented a new idea about the before, during, and after concept. What Dean and Joe came up with was, "W*hat does a person deserve before, during, and after becoming a customer?*"

By rephrasing the question, each component carries a new sense of meaning toward the long-lasting relationship you have with your customers. Each component is essential to creating a thriving business. But how does this have anything to do with your story and marketing funnel? It has *everything* to do with it. I will explain...

Before...What does a prospect deserve before they become your customer? Why are they attracted to your story in the first place? Are they in pain, are they suffering, do they have a problem that only you can solve? What can you offer them in the beginning to intrigue them to take action on your irresistible giveaway?

During...What does that prospect deserve as they become a customer by making their first purchase with you? What additional value can be delivered to give them the ultimate experience?

After...What does your customer deserve after they become your customer? How will you continue the conversation and the relationship after they purchase?

The breakthrough I had with the concept of before, during, and after is that it is the structure of a story. It has the three (3) essential parts - the beginning (before), the middle (during), and the end (after).

In a story, you have a protagonist (hero) that is introduced in the beginning. Then there is an antagonist (person, crisis, aliens, etc.) that is thrown at the protagonist to cause conflict in the middle. Then there is the climatic end where the protagonist overcomes all and lives happily ever after.

The whole marketing funnel idea incorporates the before, during, and after concept as shown in the next funnel image:

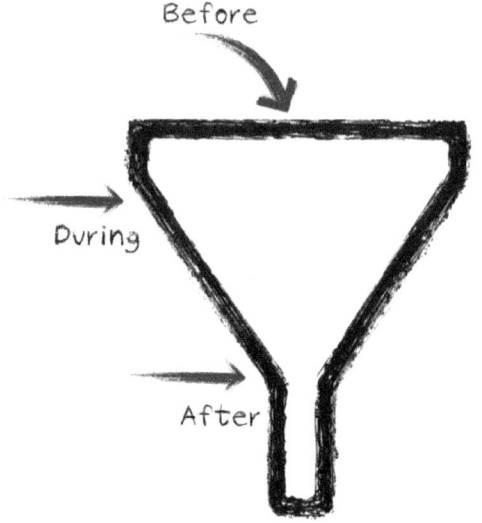

Funnel image 7

Too many businesses are focused on only one part of the before, during, and after concept part of their marketing funnel. Neglecting any part creates a funnel interrupt. If your funnel is not set up to take care of a prospect as they are attracted to your funnel, then you have interrupted their potential experience with your story.

If your business does not have systems in place to take care of your prospects during their conversion to customers, then you are interrupting your cashflow.

If you are not continually following up with your customers after they transition from prospect to customer, then you are doing them a disservice and they will take their business elsewhere.

Every point in your marketing funnel must be set up to provide the natural steps for people before, during, and after they become customers. It is totally pointless to focus on one or two points and neglect the others. People are wiser these days and they will not put up with anything but a perfect experience with your business.

Every point in your marketing funnel must have a corresponding system for following up. Remember, *people follow those who follow up, and those who don't, the people forget.*

In the *NO B.S Grassroots Marketing* book, author Dan Kennedy says:

"The thing about follow-up in general is this: Most business people fail at it miserably. If you will discipline yourself and organize your business to capture full contact information from every prospect or new customer, and then diligently invest in persistent follow-up, you gain enormous competitive advantage."

The key in that quote by Dan Kennedy is persistent follow up equals enormous competitive advantage. Most businesses are not doing it well at all. If you and your business just stepped up your follow up efforts even a little bit, it could have a tremendous effect on the growth of your business.

The Follow up Master

Car salesmen seem to have had the stereotype of being sleazy sharks probably since the Model-T first rolled off the assembly line at Ford. You can talk to just about anyone and they are sure to have an unfavorable story about a car salesman or know someone that does.

One car salesman decided to tell a story that went against his stereotype. Joe Girard is regarded as the most successful car salesman...*ever*. In fact, Joe sold 13,001 cars during his career, which is a record in the Guinness Book of World Records. No stereotypical car salesman could do that or even come close.

What was Joe's secret? Greeting cards. He sent out over 13,000 hand written greeting cards every month to his customers at his own expense. He would send them for nearly every occasion and holiday.

Joe positioned himself better than any other car salesman ever. He even attached his business card to every restaurant bill along with a generous tip and a message that said to come see him when the server was ready for a new car.

Joe Girard told a story that he positioned all over town. It is said that he passed out tens of thousands of business cards per month when most car salesmen passed out about 500 cards per year.

Joe Girard did what other salesmen were not willing to do. He went above and beyond to create relationships with all his customers by remembering them every month. And who do you think his customers remembered when it was time for a new car? Joe, of course!

Joe Girard learned early on the value of following up with his customers and it made him the greatest car salesmen ever and a very wealthy man.

Lifetime Value

In business there is a term called, lifetime value, which describes the lifetime value a customer has over their lifetime *as* a customer. In other words, the simple version of lifetime value of a customer is the amount of money your average customer spends over their lifetime as your customer.

Most business owners I talk to do not have a clue what the lifetime value of their customers is. That is insane! When a business owner does not know the lifetime value of their customers, how will they know how much they can spend on advertising to acquire new prospects?

One reason I have found for the lack of following up with customers is that most businesses do not know the lifetime value of their customers. They are so focused on getting customers to make sales instead of making sales to get customers that they miss the idea and opportunity to build a long lasting relationship with their customers and thus increase their lifetime value to that business.

Two (2) of the simplest ways to grow a business are to get customers to buy more during each transaction and to buy more often. When your business follows up with your customers, you increase the opportunity for them to buy more and buy more often. When that happens, you increase the lifetime value of your customers. The only way that will happen is if you continually follow up with them and take care of the relationship.

Lifetime Referral Value

Some businesses make sales with customers, but may never make another sale with them because their product or service is more of a one-time transaction. What if you are a residential roofing contractor?

When a roofer installs a new roof on a house, he may never make another transaction with that customer again. Some asphalt shingle roofs have warranties up to fifty (50) years these days. Both the roofer and his customer may be dead by the time that customer needs a new roof. So if the roofer makes $5000 from installing a new roof for his customer and it took five (5) days to install, then the lifetime value of that customer is essentially $5000 over five (5) days because that customer will not need a new roof for decades.

What nearly every business with this type of customer overlooks is the lifetime *referral* value of their customers. Just because there is only one transaction with their customers does not mean these businesses cannot create more transactions by following up and maintaining a relationship with their customers. The additional transactions come in the form of referrals from their customers.

The only way to generate a steady flow of referrals from the one-time customers is a strategy of keeping in touch and following up. If the average sale is $5000 and the average customer, when followed up with, gives three (3) referrals, then the lifetime referral value of that customer is now $15,000. Now multiply that with the number of customers you have and see if that does not get you excited.

You can only see that type of lifetime value and referral value if you follow up consistently with your customers.

Marketing authority, Heidi Sloss, wrote a book called, *The Fortune is in the Follow Up.* If the title of the book is true and you are not following up with your customers, you could be letting a fortune float away to a company that will.

Follow up.

Now!

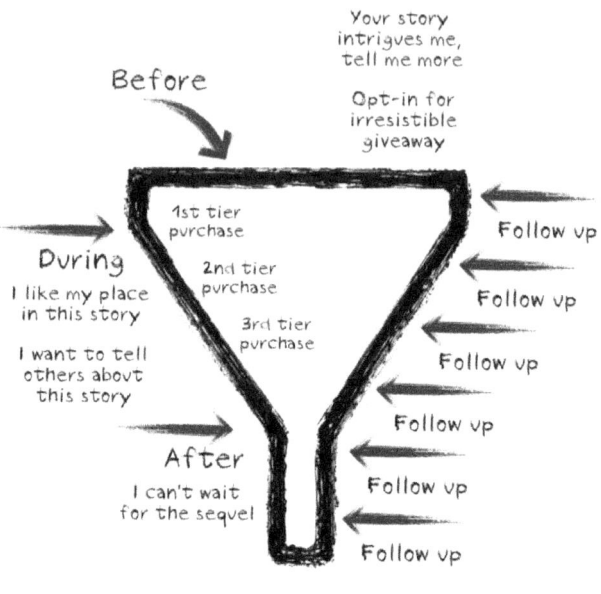

Before

Your story
intrigues me,
tell me more

Opt-in for
irresistible
giveaway

1st tier
purchase

Follow up

During

2nd tier
purchase

I like my place
in this story

Follow up

3rd tier
purchase

I want to tell
others about
this story

Follow up

Follow up

After

Follow up

I can't wait
for the sequel

Follow up

Follow up

Funnel image 8

Conclusion

Always remember to keep the story alive and fresh in the minds of your customers. There are almost countless ways to make that happen. Knowing why your business matters, why your customers choose your business, how and where to position your company and story, and then engaging your prospects and customers inside your marketing funnel are the keys to your business success.

At the end of the day, all you are really trying to do with your business as a storytelling platform is to create, as marketing thought leader, Seth Godin calls it...a storytelling *tribe*.

You are really just creating storytellers from your tribe of customers. Storytellers tell stories and why not have them tell your story.

You are already telling a story anyway, why not make it remarkable? Why not tell a remarkable story with your products and services? Why not tell a remarkable story with your customer service and your employees, and everything else your business does?

Remember why you are doing what you are doing. Tell a story that matters. Build a business that is bigger than yourself and tell a story that will endure long after you are gone.

If a story is told and there is no one around to hear it, is it still a story?

Thanks for sticking around.

I'll see you out there!

Tom J Curtis
www.StoryEconomy.com

About the Author

I wrote this book for one reason: to help you and other business owners tell better stories. As an entrepreneur, I have always wanted to tell a remarkable story with my business. Even as an eight year old boy selling candy door-to-door, I remember wanting to do a good job and make sure people had good candy to give away for Halloween. I sold that candy so I could earn money to buy Christmas presents for my family. I had a reason why and thus a reason to tell a remarkable story.

In 2002, I started my own commercial roofing company with the idea that I would tell a story that was different than the story most other roofing contractors were telling. My business would be better, my marketing would be better, and I would tell a better story to my customers than they were used to hearing.

By 2006, I had created a very successful company servicing condominium homeowner associations. Life was good! I had built a great company, was making lots of money, and decided to do what all successful entrepreneurs do when they reach the summit of their success...move out of state. So that is exactly what I did. I moved my wife and three kids away from a great life near the beach to another state with very cold winters and lots of snow.

You read that correctly. I decided that I could basically retire from the roofing business and move to another state and buy a giant house and brand new pickup truck, both of which I really could not afford. I also thought it would be a good idea to become a business consultant. Little did I know, the economy was moving at light speed toward a major crash.

Before I knew it, all my money was gone. The economy was tanking, which meant that nobody could afford consulting services. All this what happening, but I could not see it. I was also diagnosed as a type-1 diabetic, which really sucked. The next thing I knew, I was late on mortgage and car payments and living off of a gas station credit card that was loaned to me from a family member. I can still vividly remember taking my kids to get dinner at a gas station. Of course, my kids did not care. They got ravioli and treats for dinner. Me on the other hand, I was demoralized and deflated.

Only a year earlier I had such high hopes and dreams for creating this perfect life for my family. I had a giant house, lots of money, and huge ego to go with it. My vanity was at an all time high.

By late 2007, I was in serious financial meltdown. I kept trying to borrow my way to some kind of success that would get me out of the crap I was in. The debt just kept piling up and I was several months late on mortgage payments. In January of 2008, I decided that I should go back to Southern California where my family and I had moved from and restart my roofing business.

Because I had built such great relationships with my previous clients, they were happy to have me back and immediately started sending me work. I commuted back home to my wife and kids every couple weeks for about two months when my wife decided it was better for us all to be together as a family. Our growing debt had reached the point where we could no longer manage it and we decided to file for bankruptcy. That was a crouching blow, especially for my wife who had grown up learning to be responsible with money and here she was married to an egotistical entrepreneur whose empire was crumbling. My wife was a champ though and we kept moving forward. That was until my accident.

On March 3, 2008, I was preparing to drive ten (10) hours to move my family back to California. I remember going to the bank to deposit a check and withdraw some cash for the trip. I also remember driving away from the bank, but I still to this day do not remember what happened next. By the time I arrived at the bank, my blood sugar was dropping pretty quickly. I thought that I could get through the bank fast and then drive to my Dad's house, which was about a half mile away from the bank. If I could get there, then I could get something to eat and get my blood sugar back up. The problem started when I took an insulin injection before going to the bank. I figured it would not take long and I would grab something to eat right after.

I ended up passing out while driving and drove a half mile before crashing my truck into the corner of a garage in a residential neighborhood at 45mph. I woke up in the hospital and I still do not have any memory of the crash. My wife and kids were 600 miles away preparing to move 600 miles back to California where I was laying in a hospital bed. My wife the champ, heard the news and immediately prayed for strength and that I would be okay.

It still brings tears to my eyes when I think of her face as she received the news of my crash. After all that had occurred the previous eighteen (18) months, now she had to deal with this.

Luckily, I only sustained minor cuts and bruises. I also did not hit any cars or pedestrians, which I was grateful for.

When I was lying in the hospital, I remember thinking about everything that had happened since moving out of state. I looked back over the choices I had made and everything I had lost. After crashing my truck, I had lost just about every possession I had of any value. The important thing was I still had my family and they still loved me even though I felt as though I had completely failed them. But lying in that hospital bed all banged up, I had much to be grateful for. I remember feeling an overwhelming sense of gratitude in that moment. I did not have any major injuries, I still had my loving family, and all of my talents and abilities were still in tact.

In moments like that, there are really only two choices:

Move forward or suffer in despair. My favorite quote came to mind while lying in the hospital.

There is something which gives radiance to everything; it is the idea of something around the corner. - *Gilbert Chesterton*

If I knew anything in that moment, it was this: I had something to look forward to. I was only in a temporary mess. Great opportunities were around the corner and it did give radiance to everything in my life. No, I did not have an easy road ahead of me, but I knew eventually things would get better.

A year or so after my accident, I read a book called, A Million Miles in a Thousand Years, by Donald Miller. It's a book about how we are all living a story. Everything we do adds to the story we are living and telling and we are either living a meaningful story or a pathetic one. That book lit a fire in me like almost nothing else. I have since read it several times. I realized I too was living a story and to that point in my life, it did seem pretty pathetic. I was determined to live a better story and tell a meaningful story with my life and leave some kind of legacy for my kids and others to benefit from.

These life events I have shared with you were not easy to tell. I really never wanted to share them out of embarrassment and fear of judgment from friends, family, and readers of my book. But those choices I made and the events that followed led me to write, The Story Economy. I love being an entrepreneur. I love the freedom I feel from it and that I am making a contribution to this world. I feel like I am following in the foot steps of great explorers that discovered new worlds and invented marvelous things. I want others to feel what that's like and experience the joy and exhilaration that comes from entrepreneurship and owning your own business.

I turned forty (40) years old recently and I made a goal on

that day to help create 100,000 entrepreneurs by the time I turn 50. So this book is the starting point of that goal and I will follow it up with other books and training courses as well as my podcast called, Entrepreneur Jam. If you already own a business, I hope you are determined to tell a remarkable story. If you are just starting out, I hope I can assist you in telling your story.

My wife and my kids and I are now back living in Southern California. I love our adventures together more than anything. If I am not doing something crazy with them, then fly fishing on a river somewhere in the Rockies is where you can find me.